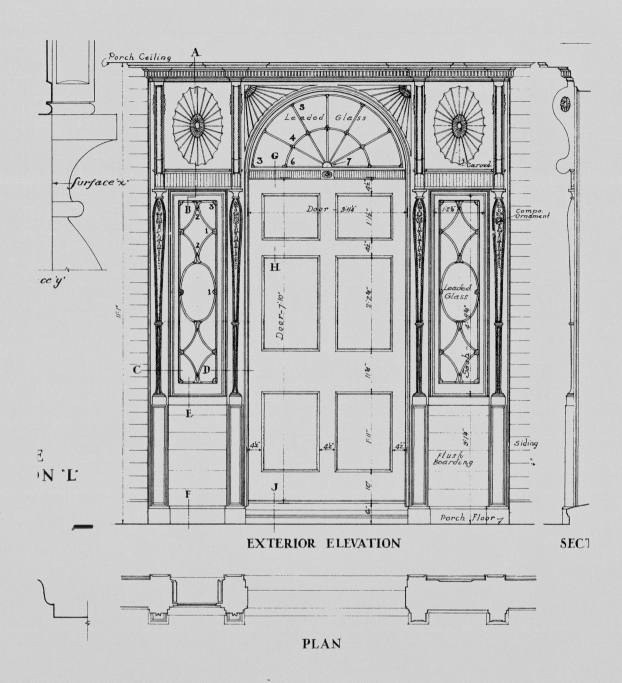

Porch Ceiling

A

surface 'x'

ce 'y'

N 'L'

Leaded Glass

5

4

3 G 6   7

Carved

Compo.
Ornament

B
2   3
1
2
1

Door - 3·11¼"

1·11½"   1·2¾"

Door - 7·10"   2·2¼"   Leaded
Glass
Scale - 4·2¼"

H

4½"

C   D

E

11¾"

F   J

4½"   4½"   1·11"   4½"

3·¼"

Siding

Flush
Boarding

6·10"

Porch Floor

EXTERIOR ELEVATION   SECT

PLAN

MAIN ENTRANCE

GRACIE MANSION
CARL SCHURZ PARK
Eighty-Eighth Street & East End Avenue N.Y.C.
Formerly
The Country Seat of Archibald Gracie Esq.

EVATION : ½"-1' 0"   PROFILES ARE FULL SIZE   EXTERI

Gracie Mansion

A Celebration of New York City's Mayoral Residence

By Ellen Stern

Rizzoli

First published in the United States of America in 2005 by

Rizzoli International Publications, Inc.

300 Park Avenue South, New York, NY 10010

www.rizzoliusa.com

2005 2006 2007 2008 2009 / 10 9   8   7   6   5   4   3   2   1

Design by Thomas Whitridge/Ink, Inc.

Printed in China.

ISBN: 0-8478-2562-0

Library of Congress Catalog Control Number: 2003104764

ILLUSTRATION OPPOSITE TITLE PAGE AND ON PAGE 6:
Details from record drawings of Gracie Mansion prepared by
the Department of Parks, City of New York, in 1935.

In Memory of Mary Lindsay

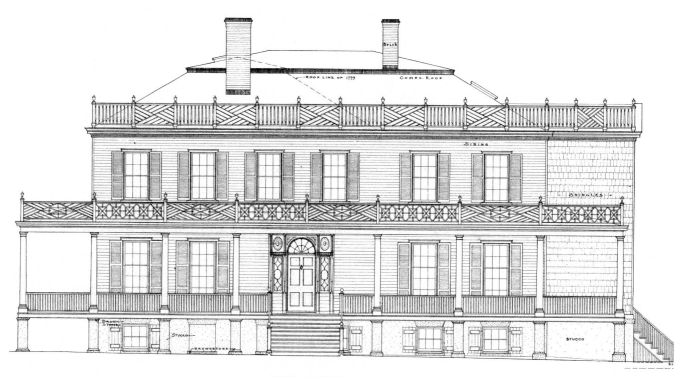

~ FLOOR HEIGHTS ∞
BASEMENT TO FIRST FLOOR, 9'-0"
FIRST FLOOR TO SECOND FLOOR: 12'-1" & 13'-0"
SECOND FLOOR TO CEILING: 10'-0"

East Elevation of Gracie Mansion,
a record drawing done by the Parks
Department in 1935.

Contents

Foreword

SINCE I BECAME MAYOR in 2002, I have had the privilege and pleasure of welcoming many of my fellow New Yorkers and other distinguished guests to Gracie Mansion.

I refer to Gracie Mansion as the "People's House" because you might say, it "belongs" to all 8.1 million New Yorkers. In addition to its ceremonial uses, Gracie hosts City employees, for whom it is used as a meeting center, thousands of school children, and members of the public who attend tours.

Gracie Mansion has had a long and rich history since merchant and shipowner Archibald Gracie built it in 1799 as his country residence. It served as the first home of the Museum of the City of New York before it became the official residence of the Mayor. Many important figures—including Washington Irving, Eleanor Roosevelt, and Nelson Mandela—have crossed its threshold. It remains one of the oldest surviving Federal-style wood structures in Manhattan, and is home to a collection of historic furnishings, works of art, and decorative objects that convey the City's transformation from a bustling seaport to the capital of the world.

Gracie Mansion's distinguished history is brought to life in this engaging book by Ellen Stern. I thank Ellen and Rizzoli for their commitment to this publication. I am delighted that the book describes the recent restoration done under the direction of Jamie Drake with the generous support of many civic-minded New Yorkers. I would also like to recognize the ongoing work of the Gracie Mansion Conservancy, the private not-for-profit corporation established in 1981 to preserve and maintain Gracie Mansion and provide educational services.

I invite you to visit the "People's House" and to take as much pride as we do in the role it plays in our history and in our future.

Michael R. Bloomberg
Mayor of the City of New York

Detail of the main stairway
in the entrance hall, from a
record drawing prepared
by the Department of Parks
in 1935.

Hell Gate, 1775:
the view from Jacob Walton's
property at Horn's Hook,
from an engraving by
W. A. Williams for the
London Magazine in 1778.

Preface

GRACIE MANSION, an exquisite relic and unique political showcase, has come full circle. Built over two hundred years ago by Archibald Gracie as a country retreat in which to entertain the noble and notable of his day, it has been splendidly restored by Mayor Michael R. Bloomberg as a place in which to entertain the people of today, including the many city workers who contribute so much to New York's well-being.

As the mayor's home-away-from-City Hall, Gracie Mansion is the scene of breakfast meetings, brain-storming sessions, high-noon press conferences, and all-night pow-wows... as well as awards ceremonies, dinner parties, receptions, and photo ops of every variety. Located on two acres within Carl Schurz Park, the mansion is under the jurisdiction of the Mayor's Office (which handles household expenses) and the Department of Parks and Recreation (the house and grounds) in partnership with the Gracie Mansion Conservancy, a not-for-profit corporation that was established in 1981 to maintain its historical and aesthetic integrity.

Gracie Mansion was designated a New York City landmark in 1966, and is a member of the Historic House Trust of New York City. Situated on East End Avenue at Eighty-eighth Street, seven miles north of City Hall, this is one of three remaining Federal-style houses in New York (Hamilton Grange and Morris-Jumel Mansion being the others) and is the last of the superb country houses that once dressed the shore of the East River. Strolling across the lawn or veranda, a visitor can almost recapture the bucolic contentment of that other time.

Gracie Mansion has long been a tourist attraction and a national treasure. This is a tribute to its place in New York and in history.

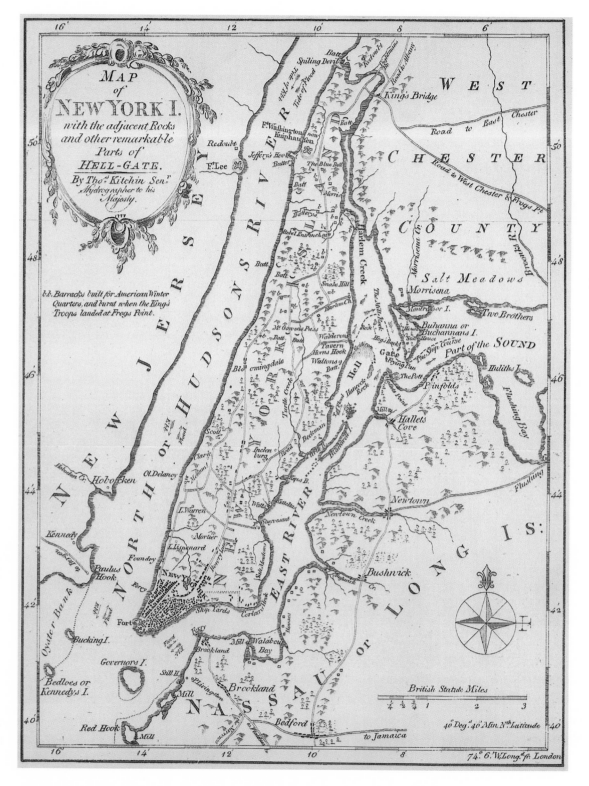

Map of New York I. with the adjacent Rocks and other remarkable Parts of Hell-Gate by Thomas Kitchin Sr., c. 1776. "Walderon's Tavern" refers either to a structure on former Waldron land or to the Walton house after being seized by British soldiers.

View of the Opening of Our Battery's at Hell Gate, upon the Rebel Works at Walton's House, as seen from Long Island, in a watercolor by British engineer Archibald Robertson dated September 8, 1776. Walton's house (at left) appears to soar above the ramparts.

The Merchants

A LONG TIME AGO, before Boy Scouts camped out on the lawn, picketers marched on the driveway, and Woody Allen filmed Ed Koch in the ballroom, soldiers of the Revolutionary War covered the very same ground. A long, long time ago, before Robert F. Wagner and David Dinkins were meeting the press, before Marie LaGuardia and Mary Lindsay were sorting the laundry, a Dutchman with a land grant was tending fields of barley, oats, and rye. For over 350 years, this idyllic site on one of the widest stretches of Manhattan has served as an extraordinary stage.

On the spot where today's mayors are given lodging by the City of New York, a carpenter named Sybout Claessen was given fifteen morgens (thirty acres) by the town of Nieuw Amsterdam in June of 1646. He named the land Horn's Hook (which would also be known as Hoorn's Hoeck, Horen Hook, and even Harris' Hook) after his birthplace on the Zuyder Zee, for it was a promontory running down to the East River with a lovely view of Long Island. Claessen already owned two lots downtown near the crowded tip of Manhattan, where he maintained a house and garden. With two partners, he operated a sawmill on Nutten (now Governors) Island. Pausing here, he could hardly have envisioned the Hell Gate or Triborough bridges that now span the horizon, but surely he knew Hell Gate, that treacherous churn out front where the East River meets Long Island Sound, causing catastrophe for barges and boats.

Over the centuries, stylists have described Hell Gate with near-Homeric awe, their pens fueled by purple ink. In *Hell Gate and Horen Hook*, a privately published booklet of 1900, Mrs. John King Van Rensselaer—who happened to be a great-granddaughter of Archibald Gracie—warned: "woe be it to the ship that was caught off Horen hook when the opposing tides met there and dashed madly in the air, foaming and sprinkling the rocks, running wildly away from them, and then attacking them with rainbowed hued spray, for vessels are then tossed about as if made of paper by a

child, so are frequently wrecked on the sharp pointed rocks, and leave their bones as tributes to Hell gate."

While Claessen tilled his soil, another man began staking his own claim. Resolved Waldron, a prestigious émigré from the Netherlands, arrived in 1654 and settled in upper Manhattan. He helped establish the village of Nieuw Haarlem (now Harlem), and, true to his name, eventually acquired Claessen's farm and nearly everything else in his path. Upon Waldron's demise in 1690, his holdings apparently passed on to several grown children, including daughter Ruth, who had married into the prominent Delameter family. Around 1712, 115 acres were sold to Resolved's son, Samuel. Samuel bequeathed the land to a son, Johannes, upon whose death it went to another son, William.

When William Waldron died in 1769, his heirs divided his real estate. One especially nice parcel went to Jacob Walton, a wealthy Flatbush merchant who was also a politician and a founder of the New York Chamber of Commerce. On Sep-

tember 18, 1770, Walton purchased 6¾ acres (which would reach from today's Eighty-sixth Street to Eighty-ninth) for £438, 8 shillings; in October, he bought four acres more.

Eleven acres at Horn's Hook: This is the plot of our story.

Walton knew an optimal site when he saw one, and he soon built a pretty frame house with mansard roof and double chimneys. He named his estate Belview and settled in with his young wife, Polly. Intriguingly, Polly's uncle, John Cruger, had been the mayor of New York from 1739 to 1744 and her cousin, John Cruger Jr., the mayor from 1757 to 1766.

Jacob Walton wasn't alone in appreciating the advantages of his property. Came the Revolution, and the Continental Army grabbed it. Understandably, the Waltons were sent packing. "When Mrs. Walton received the order to go out of her house," wrote a sympathetic witness, "she burst into tears, for she was fixed to her heart's desire." But it was a smart move. On February 29, 1776, construction began on the frozen earth along the bluff; by April, when George

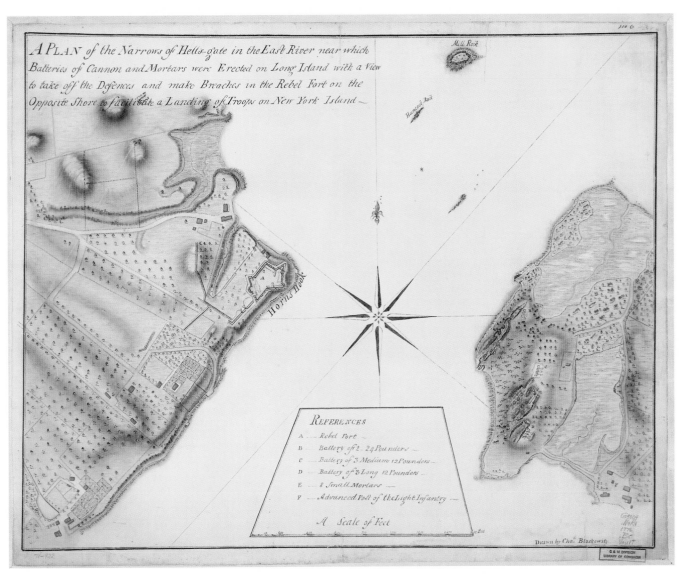

A Plan of the Narrows of Hells-gate in the East River, drawn in 1776
by cartographer Charles Blaskowitz, offers a bird's-eye view
of the nine-gun battery at Horn's Hook.

Gracie men, left to right: Archibald Gracie (miniature portrait by an unknown artist), son Archibald Gracie Jr. as a lad (attributed to Edward Savage, c. 1810) and, below, as a man (by an unknown artist), oldest son William Gracie (by Samuel Waldo and William Jewett, c. 1835), who worked with his father in the shipping trade.

Washington arrived in New York to take charge, a proper fort stood there with a star-shaped, nine-cannon battery.

For four months, the city waited and prepared for battle. On August 22, the British finally attacked—first Brooklyn and Long Island, then Manhattan. By September, the enemy was firing from Long Island and the smaller islands in the East River, and the Americans firing back from Gracie Mansion's future front lawn.

"September 1st reconnoitered the shore opposite Hell gate where the Rebels have a Work round Walton's house, call'd Horn Hook, the water or East River about 500 Yards across here," reads a diary entry by Archibald Robertson, a British officer and engineer.

On September 8, Belview was bombarded and badly damaged. Eyewitness accounts described the devastation. "The house in the fort at Horn's Hook, was set on fire by a shell and burnt down," noted Major General William Heath in his memoirs of 1798. A watercolor by Robertson shows the house

burned down to its foundation. His diary reads: "[September] 16 in the morning visited the Rebel work at Waltons house. We might have storm'd it in front, if it had been required, as it was greatly Destroyed by our Batterys. The Parapet of 11 feet thick resisted our 24-Pounders at 710 Yards Distance." By the end of 1776, the Continental Army had been decimated, and New York had fallen to the British, who claimed the land at Horn's Hook and occupied it until Evacuation Day, November 25, 1783, according to Mary Black, author of *New York City's Gracie Mansion*. If any part of Walton's house survived, it would likely have been used by the Redcoats as a hospital or tavern.

In any case, the Waltons did not return. In 1782, Jacob and Polly died eight days apart, leaving their ragged land to four children. The clouds rolled by, the grass grew again, and in 1798, a shipping merchant named Archibald Gracie appeared on the scene.

Born in Dumfries, Scotland, in 1755, Gracie had clerked in Liverpool and come to New York in April 1784, after a

Gracie women: daughters Eliza Gracie King and Sarah Gracie King (silhouettes by an unknown artist), Elizabeth Wolcott Gracie (below), the daughter-in-law whose ghost may still reside here (portrait by John Trumbull, c. 1816), and, far right, Esther Rogers Gracie, the very first lady of Gracie Mansion (attributed to Samuel Waldo, c. 1825).

rigorous 40-day crossing aboard the ship *Jeanie*. He was accompanied by a cargo of dry goods, earthenware, iron pots, cheese, candles, and soap. Leaping into the city's commercial life, he formed the firm of Archibald Gracie & Co. with two partners, opened a shop at 224 Queen Street (now Pearl), and placed his first notice in *The Independent Journal, or General Advertiser* to sell the goods. Soon thereafter, he departed for Virginia, where, with another partner, he began trading tobacco.

Back in New York for a spell, Gracie married Esther Rogers (also known as Hetitia, or "My dear Hetty," in his letters), a lady of superb stock, whose grandfather was Governor Thomas Fitch of Connecticut. "Lately was married, in this city, by the Rev. Mr. Beach, Mr. Archibald Gracie, Merchant in Petersburg, Virginia, to the amiable Miss Hetitia Rogers of Queen-street," announced *The Independent Journal* of September 21, 1785. "A union that promises the most permanent felicity."

The couple settled in Virginia, and as Archibald became more prominent, Esther became more prolific. Their first four children—Margaret, William, Eliza, and Sarah—were born there between 1786 and 1791.

In 1793, the Gracies were back north for good, renting a house at 110 Broadway from Richard Varick, the mayor of New York. Gaining in accomplishment, Gracie began to build a fleet of cargo ships. In 1795, he launched the 311-ton *Industry* and by the turn of the century would launch four more vessels.

As Robert Albion tells us in *The Rise of New York Port*, New York was one of the leading American ports by 1797, when "it passed Philadelphia and thus jumped into national first place both in imports and exports." But it was still a small town where leading citizens formed indelible bonds—going into business together, covering one another's debts, seeing their children intermarry—and Gracie was no exception. In addition to running Archibald Gracie & Co., he joined relatives, friends, and friends of friends in several ventures,

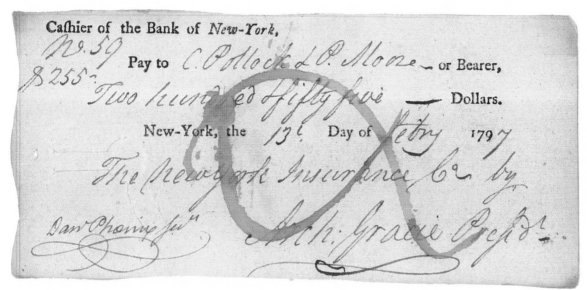

A check written by Archibald Gracie in 1797 to Pollock and Moore, insurance brokers on Broad Street. The amber cancellation mark dances through his signature.

among them Rogers, Choat & Co. (with three of his brothers-in-law) and Oliver Wolcott & Co. (with the former secretary of the treasury and future Governor of Connecticut). Prosperous and prime, he was ready to move upward on the map.

The time had come for a country place—close to others of his class, far from the city's heat and the annual scourge of yellow fever that peaked ruthlessly in the summer of 1798. Intoxicated by the setting at Horn's Hook, perhaps even tempted by the river's bounty of oysters, crab, porgy, and striped bass, Gracie purchased two-thirds of Walton's land for $3,750. "Beginning at a stone at the most northwardly corner of the said piece of land by the water side thence running South fifty-two degrees, East, three chains and fifty two Links, thence South thirty eight degrees, East one chain seventy two links…" began the quaint deed of December 29, 1798. Two weeks later, he picked up the rest for $1,875.

In 1799, Gracie built his mansion. One of the most mysterious elements in the story is the identity of the architect who designed it. Ezra Weeks, a local builder and contractor, is most frequently credited, and whatever his part in the creative process, he did put it up, with assistance from his brother, Levi, a carpenter [see sidebar, page 21]. But another opinion comes from the biographer of Pierre Charles L'Enfant, who had designed the plan for the city of Washington in 1791 and maintained a lucrative practice in New York designing private homes and remodeling Federal Hall, among other achievements. "The present Gracie Mansion at Hell Gate is formed of an addition to an original mansion," wrote H. Paul Caemmerer in 1950. "The original faced the East River and was the work of Major L'Enfant." Perhaps. Nobody knows for sure.

Questions surround the foundation as well. Some historians speculate that Gracie leveled the remains of Jacob Walton's house. Preservation architect Robert E. Meadows, whose detective work during the 1980s renovation exposed conflicting evidence, believes that Gracie added to it. "It's

*The Seat of Archibald Gracie Esq.
at Hurl Gate near New York,
taken from the river,* a charming
watercolor by an unknown artist.

*York-Island, with a View of the
Seats of Mr. A. Gracie,
Mr. Church etc.,* an 1808
engraving from a volume
entitled *The country seats of the
United States of North America.*

The country seat of John Jacob Astor, Gracie's friend and neighbor, at 88th Street near the East River. As described by Washington Irving, a frequent guest who wrote *Astoria* there, it was "a spacious, well-built house, with a lawn in front of it, and a garden in the rear."

highly unlikely that someone would have torn something down," he points out. "The floors were fine, the walls were fine, there were good windows—and glass wasn't cheap."

This confusing issue, with its many views and viewpoints, is best summed up by Mary Beth Betts, Director of Research for the Landmarks Preservation Commission. "Primary sources—including John Harris Cruger, Polly Walton's brother—describe the house as destroyed, and the evidence is ambiguous," she says. "Besides, what would the condition of surviving fragments of the house be after a twenty-three year interval between the 1776 bombardment and Gracie's construction of the mansion in 1799? Yet Meadows's detailed physical analysis of Gracie Mansion in the 1980s suggests that elements of the older house survive. One day, advances in technology or new tests may definitively answer this question."

The exterior, covered in clapboards and shingles, was probably painted a soft yellow with green shutters. A fanlight and sidelights of delicate leaded glass enhanced the doorway, which faced south. According to the *Historic Structure Report* on Gracie Mansion, prepared for The Landmarks Preservation Commission, an entrance hall ran north through the first floor. To the right of it, on the river side, were two large parlors with fireplaces. To the left of it, a dining room and pantry. The kitchen was below, in the basement—and it's very likely the household staff quarters were there, too. On the second floor, a wide central hall led to three bedrooms with fireplaces and two smaller rooms that were likely used for storage or clothing. A stairway led to the attic.

In later years, New York's rich would build their summer colonies at Newport and Southampton, but at the dawn of the nineteenth century, this emerald precinct was the place to be. Gracie's neighbors included the Schermerhorns, Rhinelanders, Rikers, Joneses, Nathaniel Prime, and John Jacob Astor—the fur baron who was richest of them all.

Astor's thirteen-acre estate, Astoria, adjoined Gracie's,

Gracie makes a pitch: His first ad appears in
The Independent Journal, or General Advertiser
on June 9, 1784.

Alexander Hamilton:
first Secretary of the
Treasury, lawyer,
politician, and
kindred spirit.

A Matter of Weeks

Inspired by the beauty of Gracie's mansion, Alexander Hamilton hired Gracie's architect Ezra Weeks (along with architect John McComb Jr., who would design City Hall) to build him a country house called Hamilton Grange, in Harlem Heights. But Gracie and Hamilton's involvement with Mr. Weeks went far beyond chisel and plane. On the icy night of December 22, 1799, Weeks's younger brother, Levi, allegedly tossed his lady friend, Gulielma Sands, into a well. The case would become famous not just because of its colorful cast of characters, but because it is considered to be the first American murder trial ever transcribed.

The foreman of the grand jury was Archibald Gracie. Levi Weeks's defense team was led by Alexander Hamilton (along with Brockholst Livingston and Aaron Burr, who would later kill Hamilton in the duel of 1804). To no one's surprise, Weeks was acquitted. He fled to his native Massachusetts, and thence to Natchez, where he reinvented himself as an architect, designing such brilliant showplaces as Auburn and The Briars. He died of yellow fever in 1819.

Ship Braganza Exchanging Signals, watercolor attributed to Benjamin Russell, c. 1859. One of Gracie's greatest vessels, the 470-ton *Braganza* was converted to a whaler in 1830.

with his residence nearly in Gracie's backyard. "Mr. Astor has a spacious, well-built house," wrote habitual guest Washington Irving, "with a lawn in front of it, and a garden in the rear. The lawn sweeps down to the water's edge, and full in front of the house is the little strait of Hell Gate, which forms a constantly moving picture."

As one of the fifty wealthiest men in the city, Gracie was a member of an elite fraternity that met daily to exchange ideas and make deals downtown at the Tontine Coffee House. His twenty-one ships and brigs—including the *Braganza, Hercules, Perseverance, Virginia,* and *Sarah*—flew a red-and-white flag, and his firm imported and exported sugar, salt, molasses, tobacco, coffee, flour, cotton, indigo, linen, glassware, wine, ginger, and gin to and from Europe, China, India, and the Indies. At his professional and philanthropic peak, he was president of the New York Insurance Company; vice president of the Chamber of Commerce; a director of the Bank of New York and the Bank of the United

States; a founder of the New York Stock Exchange, the Lying-In Hospital, the Free School Society; and—in collaboration with Alexander Hamilton, John Jay, and other fathers of the republic who met at Gracie Mansion in 1801—a founder of the *New-York Evening Post.* Thus did his friend Oliver Wolcott call him "one of the excellent of the earth—actively liberal, intelligent, seeking and rejoicing in occasions to do good."

Success invited celebrity, then as now, and those at Gracie's table included DeWitt Clinton, a three-time mayor of New York and perhaps the first mayor to find welcome at Gracie Mansion. Isabella Hardy Watts, a great-great-granddaughter of Archibald Gracie who is now in her 90s, tells a charming story about the visit of Louis Philippe (who would become the king of France in 1830).

"There was a little girl in the family, who may well have been my great-grandmother, Sarah. She spoke French, and she was supposed to greet Louis Philippe," Mrs. Watts says. "She

Hell Gate, an aquatint by John Hill published in 1820, might well depict the view from the front lawn of Gracie Mansion. Even today, there is a fence and gate there.

looked at him and asked, 'Oh, Sire, where is your crown?' 'Mademoiselle,' he replied, 'I am lucky to have my head!'"

Another favored guest was the well-connected Josiah Quincy. "Gracie is a merchant of eminence," Quincy observed in his diary as he passed through in 1805 (on his way to becoming the mayor of Boston and president of Harvard). "His seat is upon the East River, opposite the famous pass called Hell Gate. The scene is beautiful beyond description. A deep, broad, rapid stream glances with an arrowy fleetness by the shore, hurrying along every species of vessel which the extensive commerce of the country affords.... The mansion-house is elegant, in the modern style, and the grounds laid out with taste in gardens." Although he neglected to mention it, Quincy must have also admired the mighty elm that was considered the tallest tree on the isle of Manhattan and a landmark for sailors.

To the south of the mansion stood a stone stable and a dock, used for unloading supplies as well as Gracies when they commuted by sloop. Just beyond, where Eighty-sixth Street is now, was the Hell Gate Ferry—which ran to Hallett's Point on Long Island—and the Hell Gate Ferry House.

Four more children—Mary, Archibald Jr., Robert, and Esther—had been born by 1801, and Gracie's social circle was increasing at an equal clip. In 1805, he moved his family out of their rented quarters downtown and into the large three-story house he had just constructed at 1 Pearl Street, overlooking the bay. At Horn's Hook, he was ready to expand as well. With the creative renovations made between 1809 and 1811, Gracie Mansion acquired a layout very close to that of today.

Upstairs, on the north side, he added two bedrooms with fireplaces. On the main floor, he added a large parlor and pantry. He re-created the entrance, moving the doorway from the south side of the house to the east—which greatly improved the river view (and introduced a uniquely

The Tontine Building at the northwest corner of Wall and Water Streets (with balcony and peaked roof) housed the legendary Tontine Coffee House. Every day from 11 to 2, New York's merchants, bankers, and political elite—Gracie among them—met here to share views and do business. And here, in 1792, the New York Stock Exchange was born.

asymmetrical order of windows). He decorated the roof and extended veranda with a pretty balustrade. And he dramatically reconfigured the entrance hall, which allowed his powdered and petticoated guests to drift in one door and out the other at tea parties, card parties, and other revels. The dance suites of Handel and Haydn, Stamitz and Gretry were popular at the time; the Gracie set would have twirled to the music of strings and oboe, flute and drum.

But while the home fires burned cheerily on land, trouble boiled on the high seas. During the blockades imposed by the French and English after Napoleon's Berlin decree of 1806 and Milan decree of 1807, several of Gracie's ships were seized. When Thomas Jefferson retaliated with the Embargo Act of 1807, foreign trade was prohibited. Gracie lost a million dollars in this international crisis, but his wealth was barely affected. Indeed, he continued to flourish—and continued taking his relatives in. When William turned 21 in 1808, he joined his father's firm, making it Archibald Gracie & Son;

two years later, they were joined by Charles King, a Gracie son in-law, and the firm became Archibald Gracie & Sons.

Even as the War of 1812 got underway in June, Gracie carried on in splendid style. The family summered at their country house that year and then moved into an opulent town house, which had just been completed at 15 State Street opposite the Battery. "Mr. Gracie has moved into his new house and I find a very warm reception at the fire side," Washington Irving wrote a friend in the winter of 1813. "Their countryseat was one of my strongholds last summer, as I lived in its vicinity. It is a charming warm-hearted family, and the old gentleman has the soul of a prince."

The following summer, on July 2, 1813, the crème de la crème gathered for the wedding of William Gracie and Elizabeth Stoughton Wolcott, a daughter of Gracie's friend and colleague, Oliver Wolcott. Their wedding night is the source of one of the most haunting yet apocryphal legends associated with the mansion. "Never did bridal couple enter into

Archibald Gracie and his family share a shady plot at the Woodlawn Cemetery in the Bronx. Regarding the namesakes who surround him: His son, Archibald Gracie Jr. (1795–1865), apparently wore many hats; he was a New York banker, a Mobile cotton broker, and a Long Island merchant. His son, born in New York in 1832, called himself Archibald Gracie Jr. instead of Archibald III. A West Point graduate, he became a Confederate general in the Civil War and was killed in the Battle of Petersburg in 1864.

Archibald Gracie IV, born in 1859, attended West Point and became a colonel in the Seventh Regiment of the United States Army. But he preferred the pen to the sword. In December 1911, he published a book about his father's wartime exploits called *The Truth About Chickamauga*. In April of 1912, seeking relaxation, he boarded the *Titanic*. Fortunately, he survived, after helping many passengers into lifeboats. Unfortunately, not for long. Having completed his account of the tragedy, *The Truth About the Titanic*, he died in December of that same year.

As coincidence would have it, one of the ladies he guided into lifeboat Number 4 was the pregnant young wife of John Jacob Astor IV (who went down with the ship). Astor and Gracie were, of course, first-class peers—but more than that. They were also the great-grandsons of those earlier friends and neighbors, the first John Jacob Astor and the first Archibald Gracie.

married life with more brilliant prospects of happiness than these two," lyricized Walter Barrett (the nom de plume of Joseph A. Scoville, who had clerked for Gracie) in his quirky opus, *The Old Merchants of New York City*. He wrote that the couple was married at Wolcott's Pine Street house, then traveled uptown to Gracie's country house for a celebration that evening. "The festivities were kept up until a late hour," he wrote. "The bride retired with her bridesmaids, and the happy husband was sent for to see his young bride—*die*. She had ruptured a blood vessel. It was a melancholy affair." In truth, Eliza actually died in 1819, six years later, of apoplexy. But die she did at Gracie Mansion—and myth has it that her ghost still floats through from time to time.

Inevitably, the blockades and embargoes took their toll, and Gracie suffered a reversal of fortune. Deep in debt and deeply demoralized, he sold all his houses and land to an influential friend named Rufus King. This esteemed figure, who had been George Washington's minister to the Court of

FOR SALE.

On Wednesday, 21st May, at public auction, if not previously disposed of at private sale, the following property:

The Country Seat of A. Gracie, at Hellgate, consisting of a very large double house, with green house, stables, coach and other out houses complete, and about 11 acres of land, the whole in very fine order. The unrivalled beauty of this situation needs no description.

The house on the block. This advertisement from the *New-York Evening Post* of April 21, 1823 was one of several placed by Rufus King to dispose of Archibald Gracie's property. Ezra Weeks, who had built the mansion, served as the real estate agent.

St. James and one of the first two senators from New York, was not only a Gracie intimate; he was also a member of the family. Two King sons—James Gore (a merchant and banker) and the aforementioned Charles (a partner in the Gracie firm and future president of Columbia College)—had married two Gracie daughters, Sarah and Eliza. Befitting the situation, Rufus King allowed the Gracies to remain in residence. For a while.

But in April of 1823, he was ready to sell, placing announcements in the *New-York Evening Post*, *New-York Gazette and General Advertiser*, and *Commercial Advertiser*. Curiously, the listing varied slightly—the *Post* calling it "The Country Seat of A. Gracie, at Hellgate," while the *Commercial Advertiser* called it "The country seat of Archibald Gracie, Esq. at Hurlgate." But all agreed that this valuable real estate consisted of "a very large double house, with green house, stables, coach and other out houses complete, and about 11 acres of land, the whole in very fine order. The unrivalled beauty of this situation needs no description." Gracie's downtown homes, offices, and stores were put on the block as well—with Ezra Weeks, the builder of Gracie's mansion, as agent. The family moved into a Bond Street house owned by Esther Gracie's brother-in-law. In May, Archibald Gracie & Sons folded.

Six years later, on April 11, 1829, Archibald Gracie died—reportedly of erysipelas, a painful skin disease—at the age of 73. The *Post* reminded readers that "the most eminent shipping merchant in New-York" had been "as distinguished for the extent of his mercantile intelligence and information as for the greatness of his enterprizes" in the obituary that ran on April 13.

"What a splendid old merchant was that same grand, god-like white-headed old man," added Walter Barrett, who attended the funeral as a child that day.

Gracie was buried in the cemetery of St. Thomas Church at Broadway and Houston Street, but not unto eternity. The congregation would eventually move uptown, and so would those below-ground. On December 11, 1868, Gracie's remains were reinterred at the Woodlawn Cemetery in the Bronx, in a lot purchased by his heirs for $765. There, beneath a humble stone, he lies today—not far from Fiorello LaGuardia, the first mayor to live at Gracie Mansion, and Robert Moses, the Parks Commissioner who put him there.

The Hell Gate Ferry at 86th Street and the East River, which ran to Astoria, shown in 1860. The red-brick stable at right belonged to Archibald Gracie. The white building beyond is the Hurlgate Ferry Hotel (formerly called the Horn's Hook Ferry House and Hell Gate Ferry House). Upon opening in 1833, the hotel offered "An obliging host, beautiful scenery and cool Summer retreat," as well as a stagecoach running every 15 minutes to City Hall.

A MONTH AFTER PLACING HIS ADS IN 1823, Rufus King sold Gracie Mansion for $20,500 to Joseph Foulke, a New Jersey-born shipping merchant with a growing trade on South Street and active interests in banking and insurance. The Foulkes (who included nine children) would continue to enjoy it, first as a summer house and then as a year-round residence, for thirty-four years. In all that time, the only addition they are known to have made to the house was a French marble mantel in the parlor.

After Foulke died, the house went to Noah Wheaton for $25,000. Wheaton was a Connecticut-born builder with building-supply shops on Canal and Wall Streets and four lovely daughters. At the north end of his new estate, he built a two-story brick stable. In the house, he established a kitchen on the main floor, introduced gas lighting, and made other up-to-date alterations. But in spite of such industry (or perhaps because of it), he went bankrupt in 1859. The Great Western Insurance Company foreclosed in 1861, but his family was allowed to stay on. When Wheaton recouped in 1870, he was able to buy it back again.

Wheaton's neighborhood was changing rapidly. On Avenue B (now East End Avenue), the Swift Meat Company

and Rhinewald Casino rose to the south, and stables and shops were crowding in elsewhere. As the Gracie property became more and more abbreviated, the Wheaton clan continued to grow. Daughters and sons-in-law populated the place, begetting a new generation of children.

What pleasures flowed before them!

"At low tide when the water was slack we would stand on the reef and dive down to the bottom, eight or ten feet, and bring up flint pebbles," one of Noah's grandsons recalled years later. "These flint stones were not indigenous to this locality, but were a part of the cargo of a British vessel that

The multi-generational Wheaton family at home, photographed in the 1890s by the eminent Pach Brothers.

OPPOSITE: This late nineteenth-century photograph depicts the house as it would have looked at the time that shipping merchant Joseph Foulke owned it, 1823 to 1852.

ABOVE: Noah Wheaton with (left to right) a lady named Harriet Noyes, his daughter Esther, and wife Amelia.
RIGHT: Wheaton, patriarch and merchant, around 1870.
BELOW: Advertisement from the *New York City Directory for 1870*.

was drifted on this reef by the force of the tide during the Revolutionary War, and had to be lightened of her cargo before she would float. These flints, of course, were sent over here from England for the purpose of making flints for the locks of the muskets for the British troops."

In the early 1890s, as Noah Wheaton continued weaving in and out of debt and his grown children assumed the responsibility for purse and hearth, someone thought to document their fast-fading lifestyle. In came the famous Pach Brothers—photographers of Thomas Edison, Ulysses Grant, and Theodore Roosevelt—to immortalize generations of Wheatons, Babcocks, and Quackenbushes lolling on the lawn, posing with the dog, and rolling hoops...as well as a Victorian interior more dense than Sherwood Forest.

And the outside world kept encroaching. In 1876, the city had developed a small park from Eighty-fourth to Eighty-sixth streets, but wanted more land. In 1891, the Wheaton property was condemned, although the family managed to hold out for a while. In 1896, when old Noah perished of pneumonia, his family moved out, and the city moved in. By 1896, all Gracie land had been tucked into East River Park.

*The Museum,
the Matrons,
and Moses*

Early brochure for the new museum in Gracie Mansion, which opened in 1923. To get there, visitors might take the crosstown bus from Broadway to Avenue A (now York Avenue), as they do today, or the trolley from Central Park West to Avenue A, which they no longer can.

MVSEVM
OF THE CITY
OF NEW YORK

GRACIE MANSION

FOOT OF 88TH ST
AND EAST RIVER·

This long shot of Gracie Mansion at the far end of Carl Schurz Park—
showing the immaculate intersection of East End Avenue and 86th Street, a
crowd on the sidewalk at Henderson Place on the corner at lower left, and
the factories in Astoria, Queens, at right—is a variation on the picture taken
in 1891 by Wurts Brothers, a long-running photography firm whose clients
over many years included such prominent architects as Carrère & Hastings,
Cross & Cross, and Cass Gilbert. The original Wurts photo is in sepia. This
one was colorized and altered, possibly to be published as a postcard. The
leaves on some trees have been added, others deleted to reveal the mansion,
and the windows touched up.

Stepping Lively up Steps of Attainment is the quaint title given this picture of unidentified school boys in an unknown year at a side entrance to Gracie Mansion. It was taken by Brown Brothers, a photo agency established in 1904 that was famous for covering people, phenomena, and daily events for many New York newspapers.

GRACIE MANSION, the jewel that had glittered for a century and embraced three thriving families, now faced a shoddy stretch. "Its general appearance of dilapidation in token of a ripe old age would give joy to the heart of an antiquarian, but would make the average citizen blush for the manifest official neglect in permitting a park structure to crumble for the lack of a little care," scolded the *Evening Sun* in 1913. The property was a sorry mess.

The Parks Department flirted with the idea of giving Gracie a face-lift, along with new lighting and heating systems, but the *Sun* was correct: Nobody seemed to care enough to follow through. The money intended for the house went instead into more trees and shrubs for Carl Schurz Park—the former East River Park having been enlarged and renamed to honor a man who had been Lincoln's minister to Spain, a United States senator, and, ironically, the managing editor of Gracie's *New-York Evening Post*.

Over the next several years, this decorous place—where banquets and gavottes had accompanied so many seasons—now became a catch-all for girls' sewing classes, English-language classes for immigrants, boys' carpentry workshops, Parks Department storage, and an ice-cream stand. For anyone in need, the basement offered public rest rooms.

"In the branches, there was sometimes an occasional oriole, and the chattering cat-bird inhabited the shrubs which were tangled and overgrown," observed a writer named L. Standerman in the early 1920s. "An ancient owl was the star denizen. He was capable of making himself sensational at night; for this was a very lonely spot." The nearby Nathaniel Prime estate, built in 1800 and as beautiful as Gracie's, had been even more sadly gripped by the twentieth century: It stood on Eighty-ninth Street, within the grounds of St. Joseph's Orphan Asylum.

Were it not for the tireless efforts of high society, Gracie Mansion might have disappeared altogether. Oddly, the aristocrats who cared so passionately about saving it were divided into two battling groups. The leader of one was Mrs. John King Van Rensselaer, the grande dame who was Gracie's

OPPOSITE: Gracie Mansion as the Museum of the City of New York from 1923 to 1932. The sign at the front door says so.

great-granddaughter, May. She mustered twenty high-born women—all descendants of New York's oldest families—to form a society called Patriotic New Yorkers, urging that "It would be most desirable if this house which is now owned by the city could be arranged for a museum, picturing the guests who had been entertained there, in the costumes of the beginning of 1800." The other team, whose goal was similar, rallied around Henry Collins Brown, who published an annual compendium of New Yorkiana known as *Valentine's Manual*.

In this overwrought drive for control, Brown's team won. When the Museum of the City of New York was founded in 1923, he became its director. Trustees and members included Franklin D. Roosevelt, Charles Dana Gibson, Condé Nast, August Belmont II, Mrs. Andrew Carnegie, William Rhinelander Stewart, Peabodys, DuPonts, and Dukes. Had he still been around, Archibald Gracie himself might well have joined them.

Here in Gracie's former halls, the committee decreed, would be found "appropriate old furniture, objects of art, decorations, fixtures, mementoes, relics, records and other objects and collections of historic and patriotic interest" depicting the history of Old New York. Period rooms and other exhibits containing ship models and costumed mannequins occupied the premises until 1932, when the museum moved to new quarters on Fifth Avenue.

Between 1934 and 1936, and long overdue, the mansion was remodeled with an allowance from the Works Progress Administration. Then, rather than let it stand empty, Parks Commissioner Robert Moses persuaded curators and collectors to help keep it going as a historic house museum. With contributions from the Metropolitan Museum of Art, the relocated Museum of the City of New York, and private collectors, Gracie Mansion reopened in 1936. But this new cultural attraction didn't become much of an attraction. Although the crosstown bus replaced the crosstown trolley that year, the mansion remained rather inaccessible. On top of that, its exhibits were depleted when delicate objects had to be stored away for months while the East River Drive was being constructed under the front yard.

Consequently, New Yorkers came up with alternatives.

"My friends and I feel this is the perfect site to start a 'night club' particularly adapted to young people," Thomas Cooney Jr. wrote to Mayor LaGuardia in December 1940. "There is no place in Manhattan that offers *us* this entertainment. The movies are the inevitable answer to our dates. After the picture, a soda in an overcrowded ice cream parlor where the corner-store 'roughnecks' ruin any atmosphere of pleasantness.

"*Nobody ever goes to see Gracie Mansion,*" he italicized. "My friends and I would like to start at once, with your approval."

"What you suggest is impossible," came the churlish response from Park Engineer William H. Latham.

But inspiration would not be thwarted. "What do you think of putting a tea room in the Gracie Mansion?" queried George E. Spargo, Moses's executive officer in the Parks Department.

"We doubt whether a tea room would be a paying proposition, whereas a restaurant, catering to evening trade, might pay," a colleague memoed back. But, he added, "the building itself is of very little historical value."

Somebody had to do something.

The Van Rensselaer Room in the Museum of the
City of New York, named for one of the city's
oldest families and now part of the mansion's
residential quarters on the second floor, offers a
chaste display in the early 1920s. The work table
next to the sofa (c. 1820) is similar to pieces in
the current Gracie Mansion collection.

The Sheraton Reception Room was installed in
what is now the library. The delicate wallpaper
border above the chair rail and filmy window
hangings create a dainty formality. The sofa
and card table are typical Sheraton pieces.

The current dining room is shown here in its museum incarnation as the Early English Room. The Federal-style mantel still exists, but the far wall has been removed. When the house is converted for mayoral occupancy in 1942, the door to the right of the fireplace will be sealed and the hallway seen through the open doorway will be incorporated into the dining room. The hooked rugs are a major contrast to the almost whimsical wallpaper mural of a merchant ship coming into port. An enormous English hunt table centers the room.

OPPOSITE: This 1937 aerial view of Gracie Mansion in Carl Schurz Park poignantly presents the last survivor of a glorious summer colony. The tall, wide building across East End Avenue is Doctors Hospital (to become Beth Israel Medical Center). The ball field on the right is on landfill. A fireboat station perches at the river's edge.

The mansion in darker days, when a sign tacked to a post on the porch advertised ice cream. This photograph was taken in the 1930s for the Historic American Buildings Survey, which was created by the National Park Service for out-of-work architects and photographers during the Depression. Since then it has produced an invaluable archive.

LEFT: Life-saving station and a rocky beach on the East River, below Gracie Mansion, in 1935.

The East River Drive under construction in June, 1940, south of Gracie Mansion (left), and the East River Drive north of the mansion in October 1940, with an elevated view of it in the hazy distance. In 1945, the highway was renamed the Franklin D. Roosevelt East River Drive (now familiarly known as "the FDR") to honor the late president.

LOOKING S. FROM GRACIE MANSION

Photo No. 53 Date JUNE 21 1940
CONTRACT 11B REVAMPING
CARL SCHURZ PARK, N.Y.C.

RIGHT: All the city's major highways and expressways were built by Parks Commissioner Robert Moses except for this one; the East River Drive was the creation of Stanley M. Isaacs, Borough President of Manhattan. Thanks to him, the 420-foot tunnel beneath Carl Schurz Park would save the mansion's lawn and remove vehicles from view. "Gracie Mansion is still carefully preserved," Isaacs wrote in the *New York Times* when this stretch of the road opened in 1940, "and the present East River Drive respectfully dips into a tunnel in obeisance to its historic beauty."

The Mayors

ONE MORNING in 1935, Fiorello LaGuardia received a letter at City Hall.

"I asked approximately seventy-five people if they knew where the Mayor of New York City lives. Only one had a vague idea where he does reside," wrote one C. C. Coogan of the Bronx. "The Chief Magistrate of the largest city in the western hemisphere lives—who knows where? We have millions of visitors to New York City annually and few of us can point out the home of our Mayor.

"I propose at this time, when the cost of materials is low and many are unemployed, that the City of New York select a proper site and build and furnish a mansion to house the present and future Mayors of our great city."

Mr. Coogan went on to say that a "suitable location in Central Park would be ideal," since it "could be laid out with beautiful gardens and walks and could be made absolutely private by erecting a tall iron fence around the property."

LaGuardia had no interest in such an idea.

But Robert Moses did.

FIORELLO H. LAGUARDIA, 1942–1945

New York's mayors had always lived at home, and the venue varied greatly—from the downtown wood dwelling of Thomas Willett, the city's first mayor in 1665, to the Gramercy Park Greek Revival rowhouse of James Harper, the sixty-fifth, to the uptown sixth-floor apartment of Fiorello LaGuardia, the ninety-ninth. In the exalted opinion of the increasingly powerful Parks Commissioner Robert Moses, such inconsistency would never do. He was determined to pluck the "Little Flower," as LaGuardia was known, from his flat and plant him in a palace.

Fiorello LaGuardia stamped his foot. Since the 1920s, he had lived in six rooms very comfortably at 1274 Fifth Avenue. Since 1933, he had served his city just fine, without antiques and fancy trappings. Why should he move now? The mayor's role demanded dignity, Moses insisted, and he should have a permanent residence like the White House or Governor's Mansion.

In 1936, Moses proposed a site befitting his grand plan: the

Schwab's Residence, Riverside Drive, New York.

"What! Me in *that*?" Fiorello LaGuardia (opposite) squalled when Robert Moses proposed the Schwab mansion (above) as the mayor's official residence. Designed by architect Maurice Hébert and constructed in 1905–6, this fabulous castle and its gardens occupied the entire block from Riverside Drive to West End Avenue, 73rd to 74th Streets. Demolished in 1948, it was replaced by Schwab House, a brick apartment building.

neo-Loire Valley chateau on Riverside Drive at Seventy-third Street that had been built in 1905 by U.S. Steel's first president, Charles M. Schwab, and was now being offered as a gift to the city. But Fiorello LaGuardia, man of the people, scoffed at the turreted seventy-five-room showplace. "What! Me in *that*?" he cried, as indignant as George Washington refusing the crown.

Which, for a while, kept the commissioner at bay.

Then in June 1941, a creative query appeared in Moses's mailbag, regarding the fate of Gracie Mansion.

"The writer possesses sufficient historic material in the way of furniture, relics, books, prints, etc. to make a historic museum of any house the city is trying to preserve," stated a local named George J. Steidler. "I don't want to sell or give away. I will loan indefinitely on condition that my wife & I can live rent free under the same roof with our things."

Such an offer was not viable, of course. But Moses perked up, and back to the mayor he went. As a museum, he argued, the mansion was a flop and, even worse, was vulnerable to vandals. Finally, after appealing to LaGuardia's sense of practicality, if not his vanity, Moses won the mayor over.

When LaGuardia gave in, Moses got rolling. The mansion had been patched and painted with minimal expense several times since 1927, but now it was time to splurge. On November 8, 1941, Moses sent LaGuardia a rundown: The city would pay $10,000 for alterations on the house, $10,000 to construct a proper entrance and fence, and $5,000 for draperies, rugs, and furniture in the public rooms. As further inducement, Moses added that he would also be ousting the superintendent of Carl Schurz Park from his quarters on the second floor and eliminating the public comfort station in the basement.

Miss Adeline K. Gracie
192 E. 75th Street
New York City

Your Honor the Mayor.

Dear Mr. Mayor,

As the last descendant of Archibald Gracie who built Gracie Mansion in 1799, I feel that I would like to send you a few lines to express my sincere wish that you will accept the present plan of using the Gracie Mansion as the official home of the Mayor of New York.

It seems to me that this historic house would be the most appropriate place for the head of the largest city in the world.

The tradition of early New York life connected with the Mansion, is in harmony with the dignity of the Office of Mayor.

In addition, you have done so much for the development and beautifying of this City, you are aptly suited to be the first one to occupy my old home.

This letter comes to you as an expression from one of the original Gracie family.

Hoping that this worthy plan be carried out.

With best regards to you and your family –

Sincerely yours,

(signed) Adeline Kay Gracie
192 E. 75th Street

Per M. Schuffelen Trevor, Secretary

Adeline Kay Gracie (incorrectly claiming to be "the last descendant of Archibald Gracie") welcomes the mayor to her ancestral home. The hand-written note on her letter, presumably added by an executive aide, advises, "Nice reply for Mayor's signature, then send to Moses."

Moses then set about soliciting even more period pieces from the city's museums. "I shall be delighted to serve as Chairman of your excellent Committee on Furnishing the Gracie Mansion," responded Francis Henry Taylor, director of the Metropolitan Museum of Art. Realizing that Taylor's colleagues at the Museum of the City of New York and the Brooklyn Museum would be equally delighted to participate, Moses memoed an underling, "Is there any chance that we could get along without the $5,000 appropriation for furnishing the Gracie Mansion? It looked the other day as though we might get most of the missing things from the Museums, except possibly, rugs. They might even be able to dig these up out of some Colonial collection."

Next on the agenda was authorization from the Board of Estimate. "The suggestion has repeatedly been made that the Gracie Mansion be converted into a permanent residence for the Mayors of New York. It is eminently suited to this purpose," the commissioner wrote to the board in November 1941, and on January 8, 1942, the board designated Gracie Mansion as the permanent residence of the mayors of New York.

"It was a great idea, with great foresight," observes Henry J. Stern, New York's twice-and-former parks commissioner, who served under Mayors Koch and Giuliani. "It tied the mayor more closely to the Parks Department, because he lives in a park. Moses became the mayor's landlord."

It was a *fait accompli*, the news was out, and Citizens Union of the City of New York reacted with alarm. "This action, though it involved a permanent change in city policy, was introduced and passed at the same meeting without advance notice on the calendar and therefore without giving

City Hall, the mayor's other home, on a 1935 postcard. The exquisite New York City Landmark, designed by Joseph François Mangin and John McComb Jr., was constructed between 1803 and 1812. The site—City Hall Park, between Broadway and Park Row—had been the former Town Common, where the Declaration of Independence was read to Washington's troops on July 9, 1776. With its columned rotunda, arched windows, and cantilevered staircase, this is one of the most beautiful government buildings in the United States.

City Hall, New York,

the public a proper opportunity to present any opposing opinions," Secretary George Hallett protested in a letter to LaGuardia. Among his beefs: Future mayors from other boroughs would likely resent moving to Manhattan, and city officials would surely waste time traveling up to the mansion for meetings.

Nor was he alone in his dismay.

"Let me assure you that I have no objection to the purchase of a suitable and dignified residence for the Mayor of the city," fussed another indignant citizen. "But to seize a public museum, however little used, and portion of a public park for the private residence of the mayor or any other officer of the city is quite another matter." As for Moses's plan to plant the first family among borrowed antiquities, the writer added, "I can think of this as nothing but vandalism."

"My family is not keen about it," LaGuardia coolly responded, "and it has no personal advantage for me."

But local vendors saw all kinds of possibilities. "We

understand that you are moving to a new home," wrote a representative of the Croydon Galleries. "If you have any house-furnishings, furniture, silver, glass, china, rugs, jewelry or art goods, etc., that you may wish to dispose of, we would be interested in purchasing them from you for cash."

"We are taking the liberty of addressing you, to ascertain if we may have our representative call on you, at your convenience, to show you samples and estimate on your floor covering requirements," proposed the firm of C. H. Pepper Inc.

"Last spring we furnished aluminum frame insect screen equipment for the White House, Washington, D.C. and find that they were very pleased because of its strength, non-staining qualities, and attractive appearance. We still have some aluminum frame screen stock and aluminum wire on hand," pledged the Orange Screen Company of Maplewood, New Jersey.

"We understand that you are planning to move to a new apartment [*sic*], and we wish to offer you our services in connection therewith," read a peculiarly uninformed letter from Weissberger Moving & Storage.

And so on.

Renovations, undertaken by a WPA crew, began in January 1942. In April, the *New York Times* reported that work was "progressing despite priorities on construction materials" and "delays in obtaining metals," but that the house would be ready for the LaGuardias "well before Summer arrives."

Or close enough. On May 21, the Department of Parks announced the completion of work on the mansion and its immediate surroundings in Carl Schurz Park. And on May 26, the LaGuardias moved in—all except for the mayor himself, who happened to be out of town.

"Mrs. Fiorello H. LaGuardia fussed busily about her apartment at 1274 Fifth Ave. today, packing glassware, books and linen, supervising the removal of crates and baskets and having the customary toil and trouble of moving day,"

reported New York's *World-Telegram*. "The Mayor, however, was nowhere around. He left last night for a three day trip to Canada, where he will attend meetings until Thursday. By then the LaGuardias should be fairly well moved into their new home, Gracie Mansion."

Indeed. On that Tuesday in late May, as neighborhood mothers and children peered through the new iron fence, painters applied their final dabs to the mansion's exterior, Parks Department crews finished resodding the lawn, the press shouted for her attention, and a contingent of cops stood guard at the gates, Marie LaGuardia was driven into the grounds by a lady friend at 12:30 p.m. Next to appear was Juanita, the family cook, lugging pots and pans. Then came a Columbia Storage Warehouse van with three thousand pounds of household goods, which, the *Daily Mirror* revealed, even included two boxes of macaroni. On Wednesday, three vans would deliver the furniture. The big question in every reporter's notebook: How would Mrs. LaGuardia

After breakfast, Fiorello LaGuardia and an aide depart Gracie Mansion for City Hall.

blend her modest maple with eighteenth-century museum pieces? The answer: Most of hers would be stored in the attic and basement.

The family's new routine quickly evolved. Every morning at 8:30, the mayor would leave the mansion for City Hall in a police prowl car. Arriving home at 7:30 in the evening, he'd flip on the radio for music and the news, and spend a bit of time with his son Eric and daughter Jean. After dinner in the dining room—a scene clearly visible to pedestrians outside—the LaGuardias would retire to their family quarters upstairs. The mayor would work until 11 p.m., and then read himself to sleep with pulp Westerns.

With respect to wartime sobriety and a tight budget, the LaGuardias kept public functions to a minimum—although on weekend evenings, the mayor loved donning a chef's hat and cooking chicken, steak, and his famous peasant soup for friends. He also "loved staying home and playing cards," Marie later told *New York Post* columnist Cindy Adams. "His

favorite was Russian Bank, which he always won because he always cheated."

For the first first lady at Gracie Mansion, life was far more work than play. She scrubbed the floors herself, waged a losing battle with cockroaches, and remained on constant display. No move went unnoticed, from walking Mac, the pet Scottie, in the park to hanging out the family's laundry in the yard. Only off-season could she escape the public eye, when the LaGuardias relocated to the "Summer City Hall" up in the Bronx, in the historic Bartow Mansion (now called the Bartow-Pell) overlooking Pelham Bay. Although built as a refuge from the heat of the city, Gracie Mansion was no longer up-country enough.

As the first mayor of New York to occupy an official residence, LaGuardia relished the grit of his job but chafed at the nobility of his home. From the day he moved in to the day he moved out, he persisted in calling it not Gracie Mansion, but the Mayor's House or Gracie Farm.

As the Gracie Mansion guest book opens on January 1, 1950, former first lady Eleanor Roosevelt and philanthropist Mary Lasker are among those signing in to wish the mayoral newlyweds a Happy New Year. It closes on December 20, 1953, with the holiday company of Vincent and Betty Impellitteri.

WILLIAM O'DWYER, 1946–1950

In January 1946, painters, polishers, and paper-hangers rushed about Gracie Mansion in anticipation of Mayor and Mrs. William O'Dwyer. But Mayor and Mrs. O'Dwyer were in no such rush. In fact, they were downright uneasy about leaving the two-story, semi-detached, stucco-and-brick home in Bay Ridge, Brooklyn, where they'd lived for twenty years. Gracie might provide a glamorous scenario for the handsome new mayor—who, as District Attorney of Brooklyn, had made his mark prosecuting the wiseguys of Murder, Inc.— but not for the first lady, Kitty O'Dwyer, who was suffering from Parkinson's disease and confined to a wheelchair.

The couple moved in on January 27, and the first drinks were poured that very afternoon, when five judges of the State Court of Appeals dropped in to offer a toast. Torn between compassion for his beloved wife and a passion for mingling with the people, the affable mayor chatted with strollers through the iron fence, took the sun on a Carl Schurz Park bench, hosted parties, ceremonies, and meetings galore—and welcomed his barber, John Vitale, to the mansion nearly every morning for a shave. "He went through the gates with something of the manner Gladstone must have employed as he arrived at Buckingham Palace for an audience with Queen Victoria," observed Philip Hamburger, who lived across the street and reported exquisitely on mayoral comings-and-goings for *The New Yorker*.

But for the brief time she lived at Gracie Mansion, poor Kitty could enjoy none of it. Nor could she escape into sleep. "The atmosphere depressed her from the beginning," O'Dwyer recalled years later in his autobiography, *Beyond the Golden Door*. "The lonely sounds from the river, the foghorns, and the bells on the buoys kept her awake and made her conscious of her condition." Although her husband had a small elevator installed for her, she never used it. Avoiding the politicians and celebrities hobnobbing downstairs, she spent all her time with two nurses and her longtime housekeeper, Edna Davis, who lived in. Just after noon

A festive occasion (at left), with a tuxedoed mayor and cocktails on the lawn. A tragic acknowledgement (below), marking the death of first lady Kitty O'Dwyer.

on October 12, 1946, Catherine Lenihan O'Dwyer—who had met her future husband when she was a telephone operator and he a bartender at the Vanderbilt Hotel on Park Avenue—died at Gracie Mansion. She was 54 and had been ill for fifteen years. The city grieved with its mayor.

Three years later, in November 1949, "Bill O" (as reporters liked to call him) had two reasons to glow: Triumphantly re-elected to a second term, he was also in love again—this time

Mayor William O'Dwyer

acknowledges with grateful appreciation

your kind expression of sympathy

with Elizabeth Sloan Simpson, a beautiful divorcée, who had been a John Robert Powers model and was now a stylist at Stern's department store. The two had been introduced at the Golden Jubilee Fashion Show at Grand Central Palace the year before by Grover A. Whalen, commissioner of protocol, and exposed three months later by gossip columnist Walter Winchell, who told his radio audience that they'd soon marry. The next day, Sloan denied it—and the game of hide-and-seek had begun.

Despite their coyness with the press, or perhaps because of it, the romance enthralled New Yorkers. He was 59, she was 33, and who cared? No smile went unchronicled, no outfit undescribed, and it was all front-page stuff. Was that Sloan peeking from a window at Gracie Mansion? Did they hold hands last night at the Astor? Why was he whistling "Some Enchanted Evening"? Why is she studying to become an opera singer? Have they already eloped to Saratoga Springs? They've ordered a wedding cake! While the lovebirds kept mum, the tabloids kept the city meticulously informed.

Bill O'Dwyer and Miguel Alemán praise
the band. The mayor's luncheon honoring
Mexico's president on May 4, 1947, is the
first official function for a head of state
ever given by the mayor of New York at
Gracie Mansion.

Sloan Simpson O'Dwyer snapped for *Life*
by Alfred Eisenstadt in May 1950.
Inside, the former model takes readers on
a tour of her new home.

LIFE

A KING'S STORY: PART II
AN IMPERIAL JUBILEE
THE PRINCE MEETS MRS. SIMPSON
THE DEATH OF GEORGE V

NEW YORK'S FIRST LADY
ENTERTAINS U.S. MAYORS

MAY 29, 1950 **20** CENTS
YEARLY SUBSCRIPTION $6.00
CANADA, $6.50

REG. U.S. PAT. OFF.

Meanwhile, the stress of campaigning, courting, and controversy—involving a growing police-corruption scandal—took its toll. On November 28, the mayor was admitted to Bellevue Hospital suffering from what doctors called (and the papers reported) "almost complete nervous and physical exhaustion," which developed into an upper respiratory infection and fever. Released after two weeks, he recuperated in Florida—which proved so pleasant that he and Sloan decided to be married there, in the small fishing town of Stuart, on December 20, 1949.

Reports differed on whether the ceremony took eight, nine, or ten minutes—but there was no dispute that the couple omitted "obey" from their vows. After a honeymoon cruise aboard a friend's yacht, they returned to New York on December 28.

Did the new Mrs. O have any plans for redecorating Gracie Mansion? a reporter asked as they crossed the moonlit airfield.

"I haven't any plans at all," the bride replied.

"Can she cook?" a reporter shouted.

"We're going home to find out," said the mayor. And off to Gracie Mansion they sped. Arriving by motorcade at 8:20 p.m., the sun-tanned newlyweds invited the press inside, answered a few questions, and posed on the staircase and before a fireplace. Roses and poinsettias, cops and bigwigs were everywhere to greet them, as was a small Christmas tree in the upstairs sitting room. On New Year's Eve, Sloan O'Dwyer presided over her first Gracie Mansion affair when her husband was sworn in for his second term. On New Year's Day, 1950, the mayoral guest book opened to its first page, and Eleanor Roosevelt stopped in the first week.

The O'Dwyers' festive reign came to an end only eight months later. The disgraced mayor resigned "for health reasons," got himself appointed ambassador to Mexico, and departed Gracie Mansion on a hot August day. By the time he reached City Hall for his farewell address, the temperature had risen to 104 degrees.

On August 30, 1950, the O'Dwyers'
household goods are packed. Some
will go into storage and some to
their new home in Mexico, where he
will serve as U.S. ambassador.

The O'Dwyers leave the mansion on
August 31, 1950.

VINCENT R. IMPELLITTERI, 1950–1953

When Vincent R. Impellitteri, president of the City Council, succeeded O'Dwyer in September 1950, the acting mayor was set on being elected for the remaining three years of O'Dwyer's term. "After November 7," he declared, "I expect Gracie Mansion to be my permanent residence." The acting first lady wasn't so sure. "My own maid will remain at our apartment, which we intend to keep and which will be occupied by my mother and brother," said Betty to the *Daily News,* referring to their four-room home at 200 West Sixteenth Street.

September 5 was breezy, and the move-in was a breeze. At 2 p.m., the first couple arrived at Gracie Mansion with seven suitcases. There they were greeted by Lewis Jones, the majordomo who had been hired by the Parks Department the week before to run the house (aided by a cook, a parlor maid, a chambermaid, and a laundress). They toured the rooms, they smiled for the cameras, and they took to the mansion with little ado and even less re-doing.

Bigger than a postage stamp, smaller than a poster is the poster stamp, ballyhooing O'Dwyer for mayor, Impellitteri for City Council president, and Lazarus Joseph for comptroller, in 1949.

Betty Impellitteri stands by her man.

"The house is here. The servants are here. I have no troubles," Betty gaily told reporters. She had everything she needed, except enough ashtrays. Regarding the décor bequeathed by the O'Dwyers, she said she'd gladly leave things as they were—although she had brought along her own silver service and cocktail shaker. Would she keep her job as a legal secretary? She didn't know yet.

While bulbs flashed, the mayor toted piles of books up the grand stairway under his wife's direction. Then he ducked out to attend a memorial mass at St. Patrick's.

"Of course, we don't know what we'll have to face in the way of official entertaining," the first lady said, "but we hope to live a quiet, peaceful life." Which seems to be just what they did. They had no children and few shindigs. Thirty years later, the mayor would tell Ed Koch's chief of staff that he never had overnight guests and that "the grounds were never used."

"There isn't much to say about Mayor Impellitteri," noted the vigilant Philip Hamburger in *The New Yorker*. "The gates to the Mansion are closed most of the time. The lights aren't on much. Sometimes I think that nobody has been living there regularly."

From Gracie Mansion to City Hall, from citizens to caricaturists, the new mayor seemed to inspire little excitement. But if the town wasn't transfixed by the Impellitteris, the Impellitteris seemed transfixed by each other. "It's always an event when I see him," the first lady said, even after twenty-four years of marriage. "My husband is my only hobby."

In this photo, reproduced from a fragile vintage negative, Brownie Scouts and Intermediate Girl Scouts from the Girl Scout Council of Greater New York gather on the lawn for a special celebration.

Mayor Wagner's chariot rolls through the gate.

ROBERT F. WAGNER, 1954–1965

"Every time I smell fresh paint, it reminds me of Gracie Mansion," says Duncan Wagner, who was seven years old when his family moved in on January 25, 1954. And almost immediately, he took to roaming the premises after everyone else had gone to sleep. There was much to investigate. He also banged his drums, blew fuses, and kept an eye on the elevator Mayor O'Dwyer had installed for his wife until Susan Wagner dashed his hopes by converting it to a closet.

While Duncan was learning the territory, his brother Bobby (who entered Gracie Mansion two weeks after his tenth birthday) was etching his name on a window and learning the ropes. As Robert F. Wagner III—grandson of a senator, son of a mayor—Bobby "took his heritage seriously," says Ogden N. Lewis, his friend and confidant from first grade at Buckley through Exeter, Harvard, and the rest of life. "When we went back to Gracie Mansion after school, I don't remember playing so much as watching. There were always fascinating people coming and going."

Off to the office.

OPPOSITE: Democratic Partying, with President Harry Truman at a reception in 1959 and John F. Kennedy on a campaign stop in 1960.

"Bobby was third-generation in the family business," adds writer and friend Tony Hiss. "He knew all the old-timers—his grandfather's cronies as well as his father's—and because his dad knew how smart he was, and how they shared the same perceptions, he could wander in and out of meetings and receptions without being in the way."

Wagner's was the first administration to feel the force of television, and the family took to the new medium with aplomb. On June 4, 1954, five months after moving in, they appeared on *Person to Person*, CBS's groundbreaking interview show with Edward R. Murrow.

"The boys like it?" Murrow asked. "Lots of room to play."

"It is wonderful," the first lady replied. "You can let them out and they can't get out of the gate and you don't have to worry." Little did she know.

Duncan remembers his debut in the sophisticated social life of the mansion. "We'd just moved in and were going to hire a butler. I was fascinated. This was great! My father was giving a cocktail party, and Governor Averell Harriman was there in a tux. I walked over to him and asked, 'Are you our new butler?' He really didn't have a sense of humor, but my father laughed. I didn't know what a butler was."

As it turned out, the butler was to be the indefatigable Henry Schmidt, who would be at the mayor's right hand for his full twelve-year term. His morning duties included helping Bob Wagner (who was color-blind) to choose his clothes, bringing breakfast to the boys while they watched television before being driven to school, and serving at the mayor's frequent breakfast meetings. By 1962, Schmidt was earning $85 a week, while the cook earned $89, the chambermaid $73, the parlor maid $60, and the laundress $50. Staff salaries were paid, of course, by the city.

While her husband was dealing with a long newspaper strike, the controversial razing of Pennsylvania Station, and the rigors of urban renewal, Mrs. Wagner was holding four luncheons, teas, or receptions a week. So many canapés, so many caveats! Kings and Boy Scouts, club women and crooners—they all sought entrée and attention.

Summers, the first family slipped off to Islip, Long Island. In springtime and fall, the boys rode their bikes around Gracie's driveway, played softball on the lawn, and flew kites with their father (although Bobby was more of a reader than an athlete). At Christmas, carolers stood at the bottom of the front steps and sang to the Wagners, who stood above. The Parks Department set up Christmas trees in the reception hall or the library, and decorated them. One Christmas morning, the boys woke up early and decided to open presents before their parents awoke, and it was a big mistake. "They were *furious*," says Duncan, "because they didn't know who'd sent the gifts." To the refined mistress of Gracie Mansion, bred in Greenwich, Connecticut, and at Smith

College, thank-you notes were *de rigueur*. Swiftly flew her politic pen to schemers hustling carved-wood eagles, to brilliant young concert violinists, to housewives demanding photos of her boys and recipes for her chicken, veal, and salmon casseroles.

Indulging the public's curiosity, she and her family lent themselves to every possible photo op (with a rambunctious Duncan often seen in the background making faces or scooting past). They dutifully posed below her well-publicized portrait—painted in 1955 by Willy Pogany, the prolific book illustrator and Hollywood set designer (who'd also painted Carole Lombard and John Barrymore). They romped with the dogs (Tray, the spaniel, and Mayor, the Welsh terrier given to them by the Stork Club), endorsed campaigners and scholars, even broiled steaks in the front-hall fireplace—or at least pretended to.

But accommodation went just so far, and finally enough was enough. With six hundred weekly visitors swarming through—grinding cigarettes into the carpets, snatching her

The first family says grace on Thanksgiving, 1954. "It took hours to set up for the photographer," Duncan Wagner (seated at right) remembers. "Everything was cold!"

BELOW: An invitation from the first lady, and a tsk-tsk to her social secretary.

Gracie Mansion

Mrs. Robert F. Wagner cordially invites you to a luncheon in honor of Mrs. Indira Ghandi, daughter of Prime Minister Nehru of India, at Gracie Mansion on Thursday, December twentieth at 12:30 o'clock—

R. S. V. P. Mrs. Neil   Cortlandt 7-1000

Dear Mrs. Neil -

I thought perhaps you would be glad to know that the Prime Minister's daughter spells her name

    "GANDHI"

and not "Ghandi" as you have written it.

With every good wish,
    J. Campbell
    Secretary to the
    Ambassador.

Dec. 6.

Another photo op for young Duncan, age 7, posing with the band at an outdoor luncheon. "I have a horrible voice and never sang," he admits now.

BELOW: "I was taught that a lady should only be in the newspapers when she marries and when she dies," Susan Wagner once told a reporter, but during her reign as first lady she was a much-quoted habitué.

lipsticks and her husband's pipes, poking into the cupboards, staring at the mayor as he shaved, getting stuck in the broom closet, and snooping around the boys' rooms—Mrs. Wagner took a stand. In October 1963, she proposed that a new reception wing be added to Gracie Mansion for public functions, and prominent New Yorkers sped to her cause and began raising contributions.

But, alas, she would never see her wish fulfilled. On March 2, 1964, Susan Wagner died of lung cancer at Gracie Mansion. She was only 54. Though she had been critically ill for nearly a year, the mayor had kept his wife's condition from the press. In shock, the city grieved.

Visibly distraught, the mayor sought solace from his inner circle. Eventually he began to keep company with Barbara

Cavanagh, the sister of Deputy Mayor Edward F. Cavanagh Jr., and they married the following summer. However, the new first lady did not become the new mistress of Gracie Mansion. For the remaining months of Wagner's third term, they took an apartment a few blocks south on Gracie Ter-

> Mayor Robert F. Wagner
> and his family
> acknowledge with grateful appreciation
> your kind thought and expression of sympathy

race. And in memory of Susan, the mayor pressed on with plans for the new wing.

To his father's delight, Bobby Wagner forged his own career in politics—but it was a career cut shockingly short. In 1993, he died of a heart attack at the age of 49. His city was shaken. His friends still are.

"He was woven into the fabric of life at Gracie Mansion," says John V. Connorton Jr., whose relationship with Bobby paralleled the relationship of their fathers. Dr. John V. Connorton was the mayor's Deputy Mayor and City Administrator; John Jr. would run Bobby's campaigns…and help arrange his funeral. "So many of the people he dealt with in politics were people he'd met or known at home. Gracie Mansion had a profound influence on his life. It wasn't just an architectural treasure and a place to live. It was a legacy."

Over the years, Duncan Wagner has returned to the mansion several times, but his warmest welcome came in the 1980s from Ed Koch. "You can go anywhere you want, Duncan," the mayor told the former mayor's son. "This house is yours."

JOHN V. LINDSAY, 1966–1973

Beset by a crippling transit strike on his first day in office, the new mayor wouldn't find solace at home either. He had no home…yet. Gracie Mansion was in the throes of repair. So while the furniture was being restored and the house redecorated (at city expense), the Lindsays lived at the Hotel Roosevelt (at their own expense). Ten weeks after the inauguration, they moved in.

"We did it in the dark of night," Mary Lindsay confided. "The press kept asking, 'When are you going to move?' and I said, 'I can't stand it. I really and truly can't stand it.' So I brought a mattress in, and John and I slept on the floor. When the moving truck finally came, we'd already been in there for a week. We had to be, because the children had to go to school." The children were Katharine, 15; Margaret, 12; Anne, 10; and John Jr., 5.

Mrs. Lindsay, who died in 2004, was all for playing the role expected of her (just like Jackie Kennedy, another first-lady product of Miss Porter's and Vassar who'd married a

"John was taught to fly the police helicopter," Mary Lindsay recalled, "so in case anything should happen to the pilot, he'd be able to land it."

Lindsay greets John Jr. on the helipad below Gracie Mansion. To those who see a presidential counterpart here, Mrs. Lindsay rejoined, "Johnny hated being compared to John-John, although they were the same age and went to nursery school together in Washington."

leading man). She gave the obligatory house tours (one on local television), welcomed the white-gloved groups, and allowed them to wander. But then, like Susan Wagner, she'd had enough.

"I said to John, 'We live here, or the rest of the city lives here.' The house was just being used for public events—charity organizations holding teas and all that kind of stuff. One day there were four different groups waiting to use it! I just said, 'I can't live this way. Not with four children.' We couldn't possibly have had any privacy. So we stopped it all."

Not until the Susan E. Wagner Wing was completed in 1966 would the Lindsays have a proper setting for city entertaining. For official occasions, they used the ballroom and two smaller rooms (while at other times John Jr. used the ballroom to set up miles of tracks for his Hot Wheels). But without a connecting corridor, luminaries moving from the house to the wing often had to trek down the back stairs, through the basement and up again.

The mansion had its ups and downs, and its hots and colds as well. The first lady had storm windows made, because in winter "the curtains would literally stand straight out when the wind blew off the river," and air conditioners installed, because in summer "it was so bloody hot. There was only one unit for the entire house," she recalled, "so if people upstairs got cold and I turned the thermostat up, the poor people in the basement were absolutely roasting! I mean, it was an old house. It was built as Archibald Gracie's summer place, not as a mayor's residence. But it was fun. You just *dealt* with those things."

Then the furnace died. As Mrs. Lindsay recalled, her family was at dinner one night when "this man came in through the dining-room door covered with rust, from head to foot.

The snows of yesteryear.

He'd been working on the thing for hours. He looked at me and said, 'I can't fix this. I just can't.'" The family had no heat in the house for days, because it wasn't easy finding a furnace to match the old fittings. "I figured we could handle it, but Margi had some friends over, and she said, 'I'm not going to live in this house. It's ice cold. Can we go over to the wing?' I said, 'Sure.'" The new Susan E. Wagner Wing had a separate heating system. "So they took their sleeping bags, stereo, and peanut-butter-and-jam, and camped out in one of the two small rooms. They had a lovely time, and were warm and comfortable.

"Next morning, this lady who'd been on the committee to raise money for the wing, and felt quite proprietary about it, arrived with a friend she wanted to impress. She marched up to the gate, and the policeman let her in. There she was, all ready to show it off, and what was there? These ghastly-looking children, all sprawled out on the floor. She was horrified! I said, 'It serves you right. If you want to come again, just let me know, or else you'll get what you see. This is our *home*!'"

The maverick Margi (who went by Margie as a child but later dropped the "e") was also first in the fold to test the security system by climbing over the fence behind the police booth to prove it could be done. But she had nothing on her young brother John, who quickly learned every inch of the place and every space in the fence. "I had to put a lid on his going into the park and shaking hands with all the old ladies," his mother said, "because they kept giving him candy and stuff. He thought it was wonderful. I wasn't quite sure." His sisters adored the cops, but he struck up a friendship with the firemen at the old fireboat pier, down on the East River. "Johnny *loved* them," Mrs. Lindsay added, "and he used to trot down there with plateloads of chocolate brownies and chocolate-chip cookies."

The Lindsays' favorite family photo, taken for *Life* magazine in May 1968 by John Dominis. In ascending order: John Jr., Margi, the mayor and first lady, Kathy, and Anne.

The pier down at the river's edge was transformed into a landing pad for the mayor's police helicopter (he'd fly to Wall Street, then be driven to City Hall) after one failed attempt to land on Gracie's lawn. There were too many trees around, and not only that. "They had just reseeded the lawn," Mrs. Lindsay said, "and I saw $10,000 worth of grass seed disappear up into the sky. Oh, Lord!" Thenceforward, the lawn was turned over to alfresco cabinet meetings, touch football, and a swing set.

The gardens were cultivated, too, thanks to the first lady's mother, Mrs. Randolph Harrison, then president of the Garden Club of America. "When she saw the tulips coming up all at different times, in different heights, different sizes, and different colors, she thought it looked hodge-podgey," Mrs. Lindsay said. "So she and the Parks Department gardener redesigned the plantings, which gave us all great pleasure."

At the same time, the children were cultivating their own lives. Anne kept an upright piano in her room, she says, "because I was considered the musical one, although I wasn't." Margi decorated her room with posters of horses and rock

stars and, at 14, signed as a model with the Eileen Ford Agency. "It was very part-time," she says today. "My parents were okay with it because it didn't interfere with homework." And Kathy took off for boarding school. "Our parents felt the more we were away, the less we were in the public eye," she says, which suited her fine.

The mansion hummed with life—and wildlife. Smaller occupants included gerbils, parakeets, and dogs—Taffy, the blond cocker spaniel; Jet, the black German shepherd; and Ben, the standard German shepherd, who stole a leg of lamb before a dinner party.

"There's a hysteria involved in living over the store," John Lindsay said.

"A Mack Sennett comedy," Mary Lindsay agreed.

One day, she took Johnny and a friend to a sports show, where they were given real bows and arrows. "That night, John and I were fully dressed, ready to go out, and we couldn't find the boys anywhere. Finally we did, up on the roof with their bows and arrows, aiming for East End Avenue!

Those were the sorts of things you had to pay attention to."

Not to mention those she didn't know about. John Jr. tells of secret visits to Doctors Hospital across the street after playing hockey with a Planter's Peanuts can and slicing his hand open, and after a pal hiding under the front porch forgot to duck and cracked his head on a beam. Only once, he remembers, did a kid fall out of a tree, but never from the tree house, a paradise built for him by the Parks Department with a trapdoor on one side and a ladder on the other. "It was a fortress," he says. "Solid. If you threw eggs at it, you'd aim at the trunk above it so they'd break and splatter down on the people inside. It was also good for throwing water balloons from."

Another hideaway was the projection booth high above the east wall of the ballroom in the wing, where the kids would eat ice cream and spy on such glorious guests as Charlie and Oona Chaplin (being fêted on their return from exile), Robert Redford, King Constantine of Greece, Johnny Carson, and Harold Arlen, who once asked if he could bring a date and showed up with Marlene Dietrich.

To celebrate the fiftieth birthday of the mayor and his twin brother, David, Mrs. Lindsay and her sister-in-law threw a surprise party. "John *loved* belly dancers," so they hired a belly dancer. But first, there was a small dinner for close friends in the dining room, and the birthday boys got cowboy hats. "I think they'd had a few extra glasses of wine," she said, "because the next thing we knew, they were arm-in-arm heading right on out the gate. Meanwhile, the belly dancer was arriving in the car, and the police had to let her in, so I yelled, 'For God's sake, stop those two before they get loose!'"

"What's the best thing about Gracie Mansion?" reporters would ask, and Mary Lindsay would always say, "The cook."

And the worst thing? "There weren't any worst things," she said, looking back. "We really had a wonderful time."

The transfer of power, glory, and home.

ABRAHAM D. BEAME, 1974–1977

The first Jewish mayor of New York and his wife, Mary, brought everything but their dining-room set when they relocated to Gracie Mansion on February 27, 1974, and it all fit into a single Dahill-Mayflower moving van. Everyone hoped the Italian and French Provincial furniture from their $375-a-month, second-floor apartment on Beach 131st Street in Belle Harbor, Queens, would gracefully co-exist with the mansion's and museums' antiques.

Then married for forty-five years, the Beames were a study in contrasts. He—the city's former budget director and comptroller—was a low-key perfectionist, consumed by work (although he'd been called "Spunky" in his youth). She was a bubbly Pollyanna, devoted to friends, family, and him. She referred to him as "Mr. Beame" and liked to compare them both to "another Abe and Mary in politics"— although Abe Lincoln was six-foot-four-inches tall and Abe Beame only five-foot-two. For press conferences, he'd stand

The Beames move in. "I think it's going to be kind of pleasant living here," Mary Beame tells the *New York Times*, "especially if you don't have to clean."

on a false attaché case made of solid wood that lifted him eight inches above the ground.

An ardent bargain hunter, Mrs. Beame announced that groceries would be purchased in nearby supermarkets, and meats would continue to come from her kosher butcher in Flushing, although the mayor's culinary desires were modest. For breakfast, in fact, he required only a cup of Sanka and half a bagel. "He's not a gourmet," said his wife, who liked her breakfast in bed. "He's satisfied with a can of salmon, something with sour cream, and he's finished." She installed a green-and-white breakfast nook (where he and she often ate dinner) and a new cook who had previously worked for Martha Mitchell. But the cook bit off more than she could stew, and she was swiftly fired. Her replacement: a cook who had worked for Jacqueline Onassis.

For all the attention paid, however, the cupboard was often bare. "At late night meetings," a City Hall staffer remembers, "we'd try to raid the refrigerator, but there was *nothing*. So we'd send out for pizza." A likely deterrent, according to the *Times*, was the lock Mrs. Beame kept on the refrigerator.

Notables fared better. In anticipation of America's Bicentennial, many international worthies were fêted at Gracie Mansion. "A lot of celebrities came to these events," says Sid Frigand, the mayor's crackerjack press secretary. "I particularly remember Gloria Swanson, who was a fossil by then. It was tragic." For Emperor Hirohito, there was a magnificent

Season's greetings: The Beames' card features a lovely view of the mansion by Mary Hoffman.

luncheon with flower arrangements featuring live butter-flies—and for the wedding of a Japanese bride and a German Catholic groom (who was an assistant in the mayor's press office), there were bridesmaids in kimonos who fluttered on the sunny lawn as if *they* were live butterflies (but actually were members of the Japanese National Ballet Company). Mayor Beame performed the ceremony in the parlor, and Mrs. Beame performed the wedding march on the Steinway.

To celebrate the Bicentennial on July 4, 1976, the mayor threw a breakfast at the mansion, then conveyed his guests downriver on a police launch so that one of them, Leonard Bernstein, would be on time to read the Declaration of Independence in Battery Park. "We were afraid of traffic being jammed, but there was more traffic on the East River than on the FDR Drive," says Frigand, who went with the flow.

The reason was Op Sail, a magnificent spectacle of schooners and windjammers, fireboats and yachts plying the Hudson and East River. And down at South Street Seaport, the spirit of Archibald Gracie surely joined the throng.

While the second-floor sitting room was for bridge and canasta with Mrs. Beame's longtime friends from the Rockaways, two of the bedrooms were reserved for her grandchildren—the offspring of her sons, Buddy and Edmund—who loved to come for pajama parties and especially loved it when their grandmother sat down at the piano to play "The Entertainer."

"They were there a *lot*," says Buddy, who served as his father's campaign manager and unofficial advisor during the fiscal crisis of the mid-1970s. While Gerald Ford was suggesting that New York declare bankruptcy ("Ford to City: Drop Dead" screamed the front page of the *Daily News*), the

Young Richard and Julia Beame aboard the banister.

grandchildren kept the mayor smiling. "My three were very rambunctious," says Buddy. "All of them remember playing baseball and football on the lawn and sneaking at night into the ballroom and offices below, which scared them."

"We called it Fairyland," says Andrew Beame, who was in elementary school when Abe Beame was in office. "It was *magical*, not scary." His younger brother, Richard, was partial to sliding down the front-hall banister and flying off at the bottom. "It was pretty wide for a kid," he remembers. Not unexpectedly, the boys were fascinated by the policemen in their security booth. "One of them let me touch a *bullet*," says Andrew, still impressed. "One let me touch his *gun*," says Richard, "and promised me a bullet when I got to be 18, but it never happened." With their little sister Julia, they also played in John Lindsay's tree house, to which the Beames had affixed three signs with their names on them. But what Andrew

remembers most vividly is the 1977 reception honoring the New York Yankees after they won the World Series. He got to meet pitcher Sparky Lyle.

That summer, another historic event hit the Beame administration: the blackout of July 13, 1977. While the lights were out in New York City, Gracie Mansion glowed. "There were candles burning everywhere," Frigand remembers, still awed. "It looked absolutely beautiful." As beautiful, one imagines, as those sultry evenings 178 years before, when Archibald and Esther Gracie were in residence.

The Beames at one of the mansion's two Steinways.

BELOW: Invitation to a reception. "On the night in question," recalls the mayor's former press secretary, Sid Frigand, "tiny Abe Beame had to resort to standing on an upholstered chair to get everybody's attention and welcome the assembled pols."

The Honorable Abraham D. Beame
Mayor of the City of New York
and Mrs. Beame
request the pleasure of your company
at a reception in honor of
New York City's Councilmen and Board of Estimate
on Thursday, the seventeenth of January
from five to seven o'clock
Gracie Mansion, 88th Street and East End Avenue

R.S.V.P.
566-2944

kindly present this invitation

Angier Biddle Duke
Commissioner

EDWARD I. KOCH, 1978–1989

Soon after Election Day in November 1977, Ed Koch received a phone call from Mary Beame.

"Ed," she said, "Mr. Beame told me not to call you, but I am anyway."

"Sure, Mary. What's up?"

"If our new home is not ready by December 31, can we stay over?"

Koch chuckles at the memory. "I thought to myself, this is nuts. But you have to be gracious, so I said, 'Of course, Mary. But I will be moving in *with* you.' They got out before December 31."

And the mansion's first bachelor mayor moved in—albeit reluctantly. "I liked my apartment. I was comfortable," Mayor Koch says now, explaining why he announced early on that he'd be staying at Gracie Mansion only Mondays through Thursdays and spending weekends downtown in his rent-controlled three-room home at 14 Washington Place in Greenwich Village. "The idea of rattling around an old

Ed Koch takes leave of his Village apartment.
And arrives at Gracie Mansion.

house seemed a little foreboding. But I didn't say I *definitely* wouldn't move in."

The *Times* understood otherwise. "The domestic plans of Mayor Koch remain unclear," stated an editorial. "We hope Mr. Koch will decide, finally, to make the mansion his real home, except for such times as he wishes to use the apartment as a retreat, a municipal Camp David. Gracie Mansion has become a vital part of the mayoral administration of this city."

After dinner one night early on, with his sister and other relatives as his first guests, the mayor agreed. "It was so wonderful, I said to myself, 'You'd have to be a fool not to move in.' I moved in." Affirming his commitment, he attached a mezuzah to the front doorpost. He then charged Henry Geldzahler, his cultural affairs commissioner, with borrowing contemporary art from the Metropolitan Museum and various galleries.

The new mayor relaxed most easily in the library. There, in an armchair that had been upholstered in pink velveteen by Mrs. Beame, he watched television, read, listened to Linda Ronstadt tapes, and occasionally dined alone at the coffee table. But even then he dined in grace.

Unlike his predecessor, Koch was actively involved in the mansion's cuisine. What was his favorite food? "Garlic," says Rozanne Gold, who was 24 when she became the first of his five executive chefs in January, 1978. Gold earned $200 a week, occupied a basement room, and was on twenty-four-hour call for meals both long-planned and spur-of-the-moment. Wielding her whisks and drying her fresh linguine in what was still Mary Beame's homey kitchen with its four-burner stove, center island, and breakfast nook, she was up before dawn to prepare the mayor's fresh-squeezed grapefruit juice and black coffee before he took a walk in the park with his trainer. Her days were filled with marketing all over town (escorted by the mayor's driver, Monte Robinson) and making magnificent meals.

Koch was an exuberant host. He held three or four receptions a week—for artists and novelists, lawyers and financiers,

Prime Minister Menachim Begin of Israel speaks to the press, accompanied by his wife, Aliza (at left), Mayor Koch, and Bess Myerson. For the Begins' 1978 visit, the mansion's prep kitchen was properly kosherized. "A rabbi blessed it and blow-torched the oven," recalls Rozanne Gold, who was chef then.

ethnic groups and citizens' associations. He threw luncheons in the ballroom for the mayor of Paris and the president of Italy, cozy dinners for three and formal dinners for 125, working breakfasts for the staff and glittery gatherings of the crème de la crème. "If you're the mayor," he says, "everybody wants to come, so it wasn't hard to get some of the brightest and most interesting people in town." One of these was Woody Allen, who in 1989 cast Mayor Koch as Mayor Koch in "Oedipus Wrecks," his segment of *New York Stories*. Another was Mother Teresa, whom he sent home with a freshly baked batch of his chef's chocolate-chip cookies. And then there was John Cardinal O'Connor, who, upon the death of Koch's father, came to sit shivah at Gracie Mansion.

In May of 1978, the mayor welcomed Prime Minister Menachem Begin and his wife, Aliza, for a three-day visit. "They were sprucing up the brass lamps, polishing the furniture...and gathering lilacs and daffodils in the garden at Gracie Mansion yesterday," effused the *Times* in anticipation of the event. In addition, beds were borrowed for the Begin entourage, the Jewish Museum sent over a brass menorah for the sabbath, and the mansion's kitchen was "kosherized" for the preparation of special meals.

So in love with sharing his glorious home was he that the mayor also opened it up to the public, offering tours on a regular basis. "I was the first mayor to do that," he wrote in his autobiography, *Citizen Koch*, "and, at the height of the tours'

The President of the United States
Ronald Wilson Reagan
and
The Mayor of the City of New York
Edward I. Koch
invite you to the inauguration
of the New York Westway Project
at
Gracie Mansion
on the seventh of September 1981
at one o'clock p.m.

Admit One

ABOVE LEFT: A 1981 invitation to the scrupulously orchestrated ceremony at which President Reagan handed the mayor a check of $85 million for the proposed Westway highway, which never came to fruition.

ABOVE RIGHT: The mayor beams as writer Elie Wiesel signs the guest book in the parlor.

RIGHT: A kiss for Dolly Parton in August 1987.

popularity (which dovetailed neatly with the height of my own popularity), some twenty thousand or more visitors passed through the mansion's front gates each year."

Mitchel London, the longest-lasting of the chefs (1981–88), shared the attic apartment with his Lab, Archie (named for Mr. Gracie), who was fond of munching the downstairs drapes. "The porch, the lawn, it was like living in the country," he remembers. "My mother assured me I'd never live that well again." Smoothly, he took on the mayor's requests. "He wanted what he wanted, and why not? Sometimes you can't get a breast of veal at 8 at night, but 99 percent of the time, things could be done. It was a great gig," he says of his seven Gracie years. "I liked to cook, he liked to eat. We were a good match."

"From this day forward, let Westway symbolize opportunity and enterprise," proclaimed President Ronald Reagan in an elaborately planned ceremony on Labor Day, 1981, presenting Mayor Koch with a check for $85 million to purchase the right-of-way for the proposed 4.2-mile, six-lane highway, "and let it remind each of us, as we watch Westway become a reality, that our government works for us, not the other way around." Diane M. Coffey, Koch's chief of staff, who was in charge of the proceedings, recalls that "It was a major press event with a *huge* representative check made for the occasion, and it took over a week of planning with the White House staff, Secret Service, and so on for what became a 27-minute visit from the president! Because the ceremony was to be held on a platform at the foot of the porch steps facing the East River, and therefore in full view of neighboring residents, the U.S. Secret Service ordered the city to construct a bulletproof opaque covering over the platform to obstruct all views of the president and other public officials as a safeguard against any potential attack. Armed federal sharpshooters manned all the surrounding rooftops as an added precaution, while the mayor and the president had their day in the sun…which they did…a warm, sunny September day. And then, after all that (and after extensive lawsuits), Westway was never built!"

But there was construction in store for Gracie Mansion. It was, the mayor says, "falling apart, literally." At the suggestion of Joan Davidson, he established the Gracie Mansion Conservancy in 1981 to preserve and protect his house, beginning with a $5.5-million renovation—a monumental endeavor during which he insisted on staying put. It couldn't have been easy running the city while skirting scaffolds, ducking loose wires, moving his bedroom from one side of the house to another, and having his meals prepared in a trailer, but Ed Koch finessed it. "I like it here," he told his town. "It's a nice place and I'm not leaving."

Lemonade? Cookies?
It's a hot August afternoon in 1987, chef Mitchel London has turned out a perfect treat, but Mother Teresa resists. In India, she explains to the mayor, such bounty would cost one family a week's wages. Her rule is to decline food and drink in anyone's home, rich or poor, so nobody is offended—and to eat only in her own home. "But Mother," the mayor protests, "these chocolate-chip cookies are the best chocolate-chip cookies ever baked." She pauses. She smiles. "Well," she says, "then wrap them up!"

DAVID N. DINKINS, 1990–1993

When New York's first African-American mayoral couple exchanged their Harlem apartment for Gracie Mansion in January 1990, they found the house in good condition based on the recent renovation.

During their four years in residence, the Dinkinses hosted an annual "Kids Day at Gracie Mansion," an outdoor party for the children of government employees and mayoral friends, children from youth programs, homeless shelters, and city schools. Adults were welcome if accompanied by a child; everybody was treated to pizza, burgers, toys, and ice cream, as well as star turns by Big Bird and Cookie Monster.

Every Tuesday in a reception room of the Wagner wing, Mrs. Dinkins read aloud to a group of first-graders selected from fourteen public schools where reading scores were particularly low. She called the program "Reading is Recreation"; its purpose was to instill a love of reading and to improve success in school. After a tour of the mansion, every child was given a book to take home.

David Dinkins, his family, and friends sit down to their first dinner at Gracie Mansion on New Year's Day, 1990. Left to right: First lady Joyce Dinkins stands behind William Dinkins, the mayor's father; the new mayor; Ann Franklin, a cousin of Mrs. Dinkins, serves Daniel Burrows, Mrs. Dinkins' father, the former New York state assemblyman.

David Dinkins and Nelson Mandela share a moment,
a desk, and an historic visit on June 23, 1990.

The first lady at the dining-room hearth in 1990.

The domestic highlight of the Dinkins years was surely the triumphant three-day visit of Nelson Mandela and his wife, Winnie, in June of 1990. Released after 27 years in prison for his resistance to South African apartheid, the leader of the African National Congress was on a 16-week world tour. His New York welcome included euphoric crowds in the thousands, a ticker-tape parade up lower Broadway, and a ceremony at City Hall. His ensuing schedule—filled with rallies, concerts, fund-raisers, motorcades, media—was on overload. Emotion was high. Traffic was tangled. Security was tighter.

Sanctuary was Gracie Mansion.

The Mandelas were accommodated in the State Bedroom and Sitting Room. They spent time with the Dinkins grand-children, shared a quiet family dinner, and had cornflakes, eggs, and sausage for breakfast. By 7:15 Mr. Mandela was on the porch, ready for his morning stroll. "They seem to be quite comfortable," a Dinkins staffer informed the press.

As were their hosts. "It's a beautiful house, and I'm really having fun," Joyce Dinkins told *Essence* magazine. "I have to look at this as home or I wouldn't enjoy it." Maureen Hackett enhanced the flower beds and, in tribute to Mrs. Dinkins' late father, planted a pear tree at the riverside perimeter in the front yard.

"I've learned that bees are not my favorite things," the first lady told the *Times*, "but my 4-year-old grandson thinks we've moved to the country."

The first lady and friend officiate at the annual
party for children on June 2, 1993.

RUDOLPH W. GIULIANI, 1994–2001

Andrew Giuliani, age eight, would finally get a dog. Caroline, age four, would get a swing. And as New York City's first family, they would be living in a spacious and historic residence with an exquisite view of the East River. They'd miss the apartment on East Eighty-sixth Street, but Gracie Mansion would be an adventure.

The children, their parents declared, would lead as normal lives as possible, despite the probing press, nosy visitors rambling through the public rooms every Wednesday and Thursday, the mayor's grueling schedule, and first lady Donna Hanover's career as a journalist and actress.

Giuliani loved the downstairs library, where he watched Yankee games on television, held informal meetings with his senior staff, and was known to practice his putting game. The first couple hosted numerous receptions and events at Gracie Mansion, including the Annual Crystal Apple Awards, presented to New York City's entertainment community, and the JVC Jazz Festival. The first lady raised more

Cartons, cameras, and Minnie Mouse
accompany the Giulianis as they arrive
at their new home on January 12, 1994.

The new mayor in 1994.

than $1 million for the Conservancy and expanded the mansion's tour schedule intitiated by Koch. But when their marriage unraveled in 2000, Rudy Giuliani moved out.

On September 11, 2001, the mayor rose to heroic heights as the man in charge of a city that was both emotionally and physically devastated. During and immediately after the World Trade Center attacks, he was down among the crowds and ashes, issuing commands and directing the response, providing reassurance to both the City and the country that New York City would prevail. Then, as he wrote in his 2002 best-seller, *Leadership*, "I turned my attention to my loved ones. As we walked in the street, I asked the police to provide extra security for my family. I called Donna to tell her I already had

sent extra security to evacuate Gracie Mansion (which we knew from prior intelligence reports was a possible target), and we agreed that she would stay overnight in New Jersey with the children." Donna and the children returned to Gracie Mansion the next day and spent many hours providing food and comfort to the rescue workers protecting Gracie Mansion.

In a bittersweet postscript, Rudolph Giuliani returned to Gracie Mansion on May 24, 2003, to marry Judith Nathan. Surrounded by friends and family, the radiant couple exchanged vows in a flower-bedecked tent on the lawn. Mayor Michael R. Bloomberg officiated.

Mayor Giuliani and Carlos Lezama, President of the West Indian American Day Carnival Association, presenting an award to honoree Allison Tucker at the 33rd Anniversary of the West Indian American Day Carnival Parade reception at Gracie Mansion in August 2000.

BELOW LEFT: The family Christmas tree, all spruced up for an appearance in *Ladies' Home Journal*. "Rudy's job is to put the lights on the tree, and he takes it as seriously as he does running New York City," Donna Hanover tells the magazine.

BELOW: Donna and the kids on a roll in Carl Schurz Park.

Love is in the air, and so is the press helicopter hovering over the mansion and wedding tent set up for the nuptials of former mayor Rudolph Giuliani and Judith Nathan. "I'm really happy for both of them," says Mayor Michael Bloomberg, after performing the ceremony on May 24, 2003.

MICHAEL R. BLOOMBERG, 2002–

"It's a great house," says Mike Bloomberg, the first mayor since LaGuardia moved in to live elsewhere. But the mansion is a public place, and he is a private man. "If he doesn't live there, he should let his mother live there," opined Ed Koch upon hearing the mayor's domestic decision. But Bloomberg had other plans. After initiating the mansion's second major restoration—a triumphant effort that would be accomplished in record time—he announced he'd share it with visiting dignitaries (overnight guests have so far included Archbishop Desmond Tutu of South Africa, Crown Prince Haakon of Norway, and Mayor Manuel A. Diaz of Miami), city employees, and constituents.

Indeed. Guided tours of the house are extremely well attended; the one day Open House New York tour of 2003, in fact, accommodated some 1,500 visitors—certainly a larger crowd than Mr. Gracie ever envisioned on his premises. And while the house is still the site of many grand occasions, it also has a new role: Unlike previous mayors and their families who resented outsiders looking in, Bloomberg calls Gracie Mansion the People's House. "At a barbecue here last summer," he says, "I was amazed to hear somebody tell me, 'I've worked for the city for twenty years, and this is the first time I've been invited to Gracie Mansion.'" But not the last. Innumerable seminars, retreats, meetings, and receptions are held there by City agencies, including World Trade Center Memorial Jury Proceedings. The final memorial was selected in the ballroom at Gracie. Bloomberg is also responsible for reviving the tradition begun in the Koch administration of displaying outdoor sculpture—loaned by such New York City institutions as the Museum of Modern Art and the Noguchi Museum—on the grounds of the mansion.

While Bloomberg himself has yet to spend a night there, he does think about it. "I'd just bring my shaving kit and my clothes. A cab could take me over, or I could walk." In the meantime, he is on site often. Not only does he pilot the myriad meetings, negotiations, and strike talks (surely rendered less shrill in this felicitous setting) that he must. He also con-

"I think it's a wonderful house," says Mayor Bloomberg, but a house is not always a home. Although he doesn't live at Gracie Mansion, he does have a favorite room here: the library, which is, of course, for reading.

ducts the innumerable awards ceremonies, receptions, luncheons and dinners (serving only New York wines) that are a mayor's lot—welcoming such eminent guests as Mary McAleese, the president of Ireland; Uri Lupolianski, the mayor of Jerusalem; and Hipólito Mejía, the president of the Dominican Republic. He also celebrates the cultural events of the city, including Puerto Rican Day, West Indian Day, St. Patrick's Day, and Women's History Month, and hosts receptions in honor of the New York City Marathon, Jewish Heritage Month, Volunteerism, and the swearing in of Park Wardens and the Diplomatic community. At every one of them, no matter how many handshakes or photographs are required, he is a host both genuine and genial.

Today's mayor has much in common with yesterday's

merchant. Both men came to New York from out of town to make their success in business and then, with deep pockets and bountiful intentions, to make changes for the common good.

Bloomberg has a notion how Archibald Gracie would feel about his most abiding contribution. "You've got to believe he'd be thrilled that his name survives 200 years later," he says. "Most people's don't. And that we say nice things about him. You've got to believe that he'd be very, very happy."

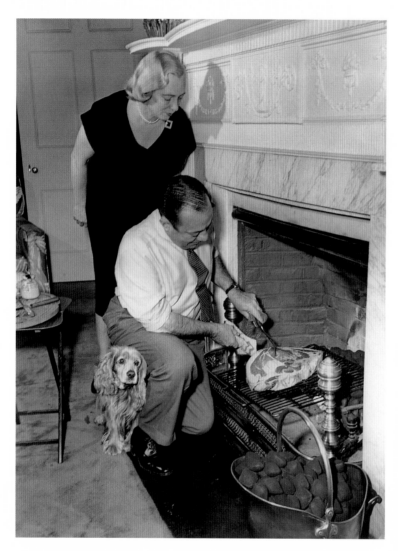

Bob Wagner claims a steak in a fireplace without a fire, while his wife and faithful companion lend support.

John Lindsay sits in while John Jr. stands by.

Jazz fan Ed Koch toots, accompanied by Gerry Mulligan, at left, and Benny Goodman.

David Dinkins and Master Wan Chi Ming do the double lion dance during a reception in honor of Asian business leaders.

Olive Whedon Quackenbush, a granddaughter of Noah Wheaton, with her faithful companion around 1890, posing at the northwest corner of Gracie Mansion where the Susan E. Wagner Wing stands now.

Susan Wagner with Tray, the family's golden cocker spaniel.

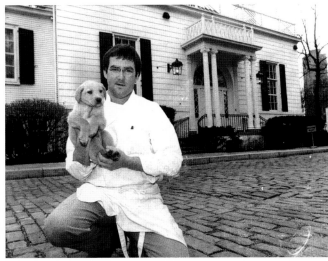

CLOCKWISE FROM TOP LEFT: Johnny
Lindsay and Taffy, a golden spaniel,
with their friends Carl Fisher and
Doxie, the dachshund, just outside the
mansion's front gate; Mitchel London,
Koch's longest-term chef, with his Lab,
Archie; Goalie, the Giulianis' yellow
Lab, takes Andrew for a run; Cody, the
Gordon setter–golden retriever hybrid
of gardener Maureen Hackett, tiptoes
through the tulips.

Traffic advisory during the Wagner administration.

OPPOSITE: Detail of a creamy Wedgwood plate with mulberry transfer showing an 1859 drawing of Gracie Mansion. This was part of a dinner service called "Scenes of Old New York" designed exclusively for B. Altman & Company, the beloved New York department store that closed in 1989.

Mrs. Impellitteri sips the soup.

Young Bobby Wagner oversees
Thanksgiving preparations.

Henry Schmidt, Mayor Wagner's
devoted butler, and Nora, his cook.

Mary Beame pitches in.

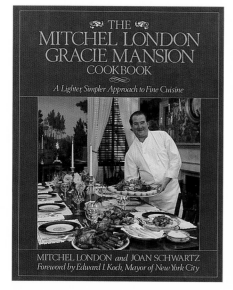

TOP LEFT: Hizzoner with the catch of the day: a 46-pound grouper, presented to him by the Southern Offshore Fishing Association of Treasure Island, Florida.

TOP RIGHT: Mayor Giuliani and chef Annamaria Santorelli admire the movable feast.

ABOVE LEFT: A culinary masterpiece from the Koch kitchen, published in 1989.

ABOVE RIGHT: Executive chef Feliberto Estevez and Mayor Bloomberg share a light moment.

Gracie Mansion on Stage

Over the years, the mayor's house has been reimagined in many ways. TOP LEFT: As one of four "Historic Houses of New York City at Christmas," this replica decorated Lord & Taylor's Christmas windows in 1985. MIDDLE LEFT: In 2002, Donald Paradise portrayed Noah Wheaton in *The Yorkville Nutcracker*, a ballet by Dances Petrelle that reinvented the classic, changing the venue from a grand home in Old Europe to Gracie Mansion in New York. BOTTOM LEFT: A winning team from *The Apprentice* meet with Mayor Bloomberg, May 2004.

In the 1996 movie *City Hall*, Al Pacino played the mayor and John Cusack his deputy mayor as they conversed in the mayor's bedroom at Gracie Mansion. In fact, interiors were shot not at Gracie Mansion but at the mansion (above) owned by Benihana founder Rocky H. Aoki in Tenafly, New Jersey.

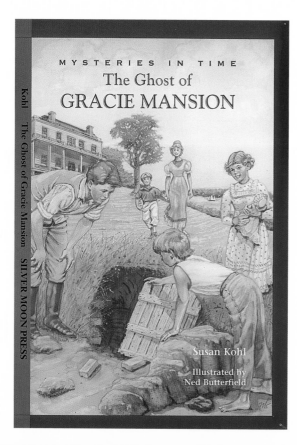

A children's story about the
Gracies and a mystery at their
house, published in 1999.

BELOW: *Spin City*'s mayor, Barry Bostwick,
hosted Thanksgiving dinner on the ABC series'
dining room set in 1999.

"They asked if they could film a yule log burning at Gracie Mansion," Mary Lindsay recalled. "I said, 'Sure! You provide the log, we'll provide the house.'" That was in 1966, and every Christmas Eve until 1989, for three hours without commercials, Channel 11 telecast the hearth to New Yorkers who didn't have one of their own. In 2001, a year in particular need of cozy comfort, the yule log was reignited—but not from Gracie's hearth. This time, the fireplace was a set.

The Mansion

CALLING this clapboard country house a mansion—rather than manor house or villa—might seem an urban affectation when applied to so quaint a dwelling, but Archibald Gracie and his neighbors didn't think so. They considered their houses mansions, too.

"Definitions of 'mansion' change with the times," explains Charles A. Platt, a New York architect and a founding member of the Gracie Mansion Conservancy, who knows the place better than most. "It's always relative. In those times, a house with a large property and estate buildings in a prominent location would have been considered a mansion. If it was *considered* a mansion, then it *was* a mansion."

And will be forevermore.

The rooms within have more flexible name tags. The large one to the right of the front door, for example, which was called the "parlor" by residents of the nineteenth century, and the "living room" and "drawing room" by mayors of the twentieth century, is now a "parlor" again. The room to the left of the front door has been called the "small par-lor," the "sitting room," and "the study," but since the days of LaGuardia it has customarily been known as the "library," even when it does not contain books.

And then there are the furnishings, which have always reflected current trends. Just as the exterior grounds change size and shape through time, so does the interior landscape reflect the sense and sensibility of its inhabitants.

The rooms of Noah Wheaton and his in-laws, the Babcocks and Quackenbushes, were furnished in a dizzying Victorian medley of colors, patterns, fringes, and potted ferns. Gasoliers dangled from the papered ceilings, floral carpets bloomed underfoot, and nary a surface was bare. The hall fireplace was bricked up, and a fancy newel post and balusters replaced the staircase's originals. Heavy draperies covered doorways, while embroidered muslin-and-lace curtains fluttered at the windows. A platform rocker held sway in the small parlor. Oriental fans, elegant gilt mirrors, portraits, landscapes, and busts added other prosperous touches.

When the Wheatons departed Gracie Mansion, however,

The Wheaton family's parlor, photographed by the Pach Brothers in the 1890s, features a multitude of patterns, from the fitted carpet to the walls, borders, and even the ceiling. Lace curtains hide the view.

A Wheaton bedroom is furnished as a one-room studio with work table draped in a Turkey carpet and a pair of armoires for storage. A tasseled scarf drapes the mantel in typical Victorian fashion.

The dining room's furnishings are almost provincial in comparison with the fussy décor. Portières frame all the doorways, and the fireplace is dressed in a summer skirt.

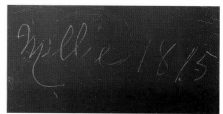

A glass act: First to be immortalized on a windowpane in the library was Millie Quackenbush in 1875. Later came Margie (now Margi) Lindsay and Caroline Giuliani.

one of their most eloquent legacies was the etching on a windowpane in the library. It is a charming reminder of Noah Wheaton's granddaughter, Amalie Hermione Quackenbush (known as "Millie"), who was born at the mansion in 1875.

"I don't think anybody'd ever noticed Millie's name on the glass," says Margi Lindsay Picotte, who lived at Gracie Mansion from 1966 to 1973. "I remember being in there one night before we moved in, and the light hit it, and I saw her name and the date. I took my mother's engagement ring and wrote *my* name and the date on another pane of glass." The name she wrote was Margie, which was how she spelled it then.

According to Margi's mother, Mary Lindsay, it was Millie's older brother who carved her name on the windowpane just after her birth. "That's what I think struck Margi," Mrs. Lindsay recalled. "So I said, 'Well, fine!' and I gave her my ring. We had to make sure it was a *diamond*."

Almost, but not quite. Herewith, the actual facts, as stated in a letter from Virginia Macy, Millie's daughter. "The name Millie 1875 was scratched in window by my Mother's brother, Daniel, with diamond my Mother received from her Father on her 18th birthday. Daniel was about two years younger than my Mother."

And that, dear reader, is that.

The Gracie Mansion, pen-and-ink drawing on paper by
Eliza Greatorex, 1869. Born in Ireland in 1820,
Elizabeth (Eliza) Pratt arrived in New York around
1840 and married Henry Wellington Greatorex, a
conductor and organist. Esteemed for her graceful
New York landscapes, she was the first woman elected
an associate of the National Academy of Design.

Gracie Mansion, ink on cardboard by Abram Hosier (ca. 1830–1883).

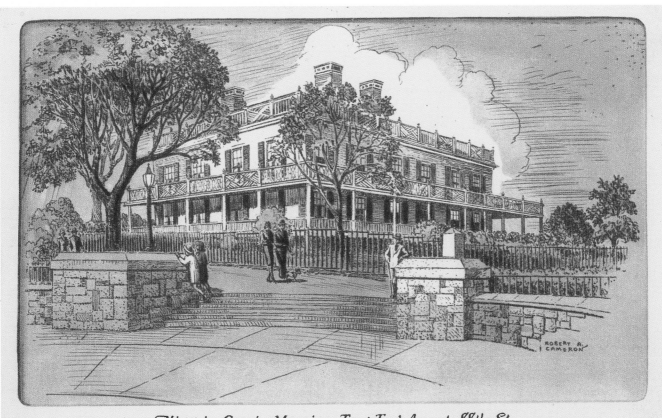

Historic Gracie Mansion, East End Ave. at 88th St.

Historic Gracie Mansion. This very rare pre-World War I postcard shows the house in a romantic light, when it was, in fact, between roles and rather unappreciated.

Gracie Mansion, watercolor on illustration board, by Rudolph F. Bunner, 1928. The artist was born in 1860 and died in 1931. Could he possibly be the same Rudolph Bunner who co-wrote *Wait 'Til We're Married*, a Broadway comedy that opened in 1921?

Gracie Mansion, oil on canvas by Isabella Banks Markell, c. 1944. Painter, sculptor, and etcher, the artist was born in 1891 and served as president of the National Association of Women Artists in 1946.

The grand entrance hall has welcomed many visitors and worn many styles. In Noah Wheaton's day, it announces the panoply of Victorian pattern that is found throughout the house. The staircase rail has been altered to suit the tastes of the time, as evidenced by the massive newel post.

In the museum years, the fireplace in the front hall is surprisingly sealed. The nineteenth-century furnishings are similar to those seen in the mansion today. The triple-chairback settee is placed against a wall that will be shortened at a later date when the hallway is widened.

The Wagner hall is furnished as a proper reception room. The fitted carpet and tufted chair are the height of 1950s fashion.

Preparing the foyer for its 2002 makeover.

Albert Hadley's vision—never realized—for the Koch restoration features spotted high-back wing chairs with saucy skirts and horizontal stripes on the walls. Note that this is an early conception, showing the corridor (known as "the hyphen") that will connect the house and the Wagner Wing for the first time.

The final installation during the Koch administration features a painted floor by trompe l'oeil artist Stephen Gemberling with a central compass star, to reflect a popular country-house style of the nineteenth century. The risers have been marbleized and the stairs capped with carpet. The rare five-chairback settee resides on the second-floor landing today. It was originally from the offices of the Art Commission in City Hall.

For the 2002 restoration, Russell Van Peterson, chief artist at New York City's Alpha Workshops, applies himself to the center compass, an elaborate medallion that evokes the days of great Gracie ships. He and his team bend to their tasks using special kneelers made of gray wool.

The finished foyer recreates the floor of the Koch years in a fresher and lighter tonality. A modern example of a period ingrain carpet runner climbs the stairs. The Wheaton family sofa sits proudly opposite the boldly carved Federal fireplace. The tallcase clock features maritime motifs in reference to the Gracie family business.

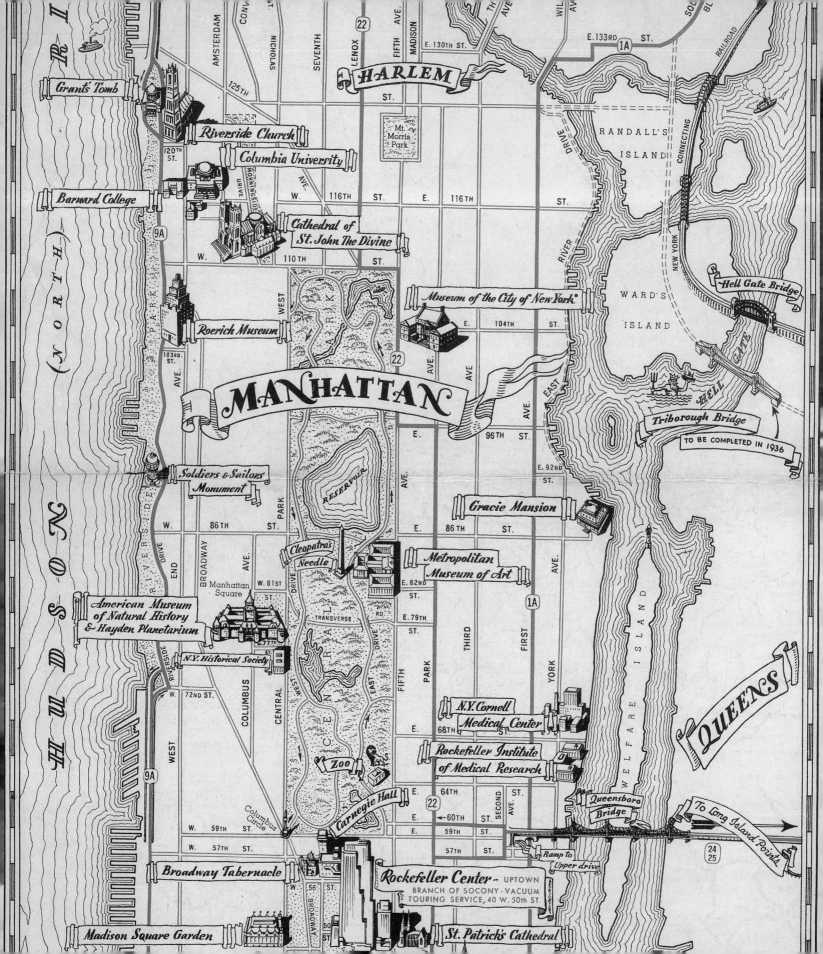

OPPOSITE: Portion of a Socony map, published in the 1930s, shows Gracie Mansion on Manhattan's easternmost edge and the Museum of the City of New York in its brand-new home on upper Fifth Avenue. Note that the Triborough Bridge is "to be completed in 1936."

GRACIE MANSION entered the political arena in January 1942 as it prepared for the arrival of its first mayoral family. Under the aegis of architect Aymar Embury II, the house—now designated as the official residence of the Mayor of New York—would welcome the LaGuardias in May. The interior and exterior were freshly painted, and the Parks Department announced that "Great care was taken to preserve the simple charm and dignity of the structure."

The Colonial, Revolutionary, and early nineteenth-century pieces selected for their affinity to the styles of 1799—the year Gracie Mansion was built—were borrowed from the Metropolitan Museum of Art, the Museum of the City of New York, the Brooklyn Museum, and private donors. The living room contained several Hepplewhite armchairs, a mahogany writing desk with tambour doors, two drop-leaf pedestal tables, and a caned mahogany settee. Three mahogany bookcases held books on New York history borrowed from the New York Public Library.

In the upstairs living quarters, where the mayor's bedroom was replacing the caretaker's apartment, the LaGuardias were permitted to use their own furnishings along with such pieces as a mahogany bow-front chest, a pair of Louis XVI armchairs, and a looking glass in a carved and gilded frame of the Federal period.

One can only imagine their discomfort.

IT MIGHT HAVE BEEN WHEN THE O'DWYERS first arrived in 1946, and Kitty O'Dwyer was much too ill to deal with swatches and swags. It might have been after she died later that year. But at some point early on, the mayor accepted decorative assistance from three prominent ladies: Phyllis Cerf Wagner, Mary Lasker, and Anna Rosenberg.

"The house was a disaster," declares Mrs. Wagner, the bouncy doyenne whose ties to Gracie Mansion make her an honorary member of the household. In 1940, she was married *by* a mayor (Fiorello LaGuardia) to Bennett Cerf, the founder of Random House. In 1975, she was married *to* a mayor (Robert F. Wagner) after he'd left office. Although she never lived there herself, the feisty Mrs. Wagner says, "I was always at Gracie Mansion one way or the other, redoing it or something.

"There wasn't a wife involved at that moment in time," she recalls, "and Mary Lasker took it upon herself to fix it." The late Mrs. Lasker, who was one of New York's most dynamic philanthropists, also summoned Anna Rosenberg, the U.S. assistant secretary of defense, to the cause.

"We were women of fashion," Mrs. Wagner explains. "We knew a good house when we saw one. We knew good furniture. We'd all been in good homes. I grew up in Hollywood, California, where they sort of *invented* homes." (Not only was she an actress and columnist before her marriage to Mr. Cerf, but Ginger Rogers was her first cousin.)

"We raised money," she says. "The *city* didn't have any. And we had absolute control." Alterations included new

Green grows the library of Vincent Impellitteri in the early 1950s. The room is proper but comfy with period furniture.

wallpaper in the entrance hall, master bedroom, and large upstairs sitting room; new coats of paint in the other bedrooms, and white paint on all the ceilings. The library was updated from cocoa brown to silver gray. In the apple-green living room, the museum antiques blended with new easy chairs and sofas from W. and J. Sloane. "It was gorgeous," Mrs. Wagner says.

THE IMPELLITTERIS' REMODELING was not extensive, because when they moved in they didn't know how long they'd be staying. They slept not in the master bedroom but in what is now the State Bedroom. The mayor often met in the downstairs library with his chief advisor, Parks Commissioner Robert Moses, and Moses's chief assistant, George E. Spargo, while the first lady spent time in a small sitting room decorated in blue wallpaper and crimson upholstery. Perhaps in tribute to Archibald Gracie, she also hung prints of clipper ships.

The master bedroom, redone in an intense bottle green and gold, showed a bold use of color and a variety of textures, setting off the rich mahogany of tables and bureaus. The downstairs library, with nearly the same emphasis on green, was filled with period-modern upholstered chairs, antiques, and something revolutionary for Gracie Mansion: a television console.

THE WAGNERS' GRACIE MANSION was homey and polite, with family photographs on every other table top. After a flock of fourth-graders paid a visit in 1956, the mayor and his wife received a thank-you note with this observation: "Everyone liked the pink and blue kitchen. We know that it has two sinks, two tables, five cabinets, three work tables, one refrigerator, two stoves. But I liked the boys' rooms best." As did the boys themselves. Bobby's sunny room had a river view. Duncan's room overlooked the police booth. Bobby's toy soldiers marched across his mantel. Duncan's electric

Mrs. Impellitteri, shown here in the front hall,
is clearly fond of flowers—from the enormous
arrangement on the table to the bold floral
pattern on the walls.

The Wagner library with its stately eagled curtains is the epitome of mayoral pride.

trains wore a "Do Not Touch" sign to ward off the visitors traipsing through.

When Susan Wagner instigated an addition to Gracie Mansion in 1963 for receptions and dinner parties, the *New York Times* sympathized with the desire, but not the design. "Inspired by Mrs. Kennedy's refurbishing of the White House, New York is about to operate on Gracie Mansion. The design just published for an extension to the Mayor's official residence might be described most charitably as a combination garage and laundry wing for a suburban colonial home of the 1920's," read an editorial in October 1963. That plan was swiftly dropped.

Mrs. Wagner and her wealthy supporters carried on, raising private funds for the project. In May of 1964, soon after her death, the Committee for Gracie Mansion was established to oversee "the construction of an addition to and improvement of Gracie Mansion."

Architect Mott B. Schmidt, who had done homes for Rockefellers, Vanderbilts, and Astors, was chosen to design the two-story wing in the style of the eighteenth century. His ballroom, inspired by the ballroom of the Theodore Lyman House in Waltham, Massachusetts, measured twenty-four by fifty feet with an eighteen-foot ceiling. It was enhanced by freestanding Corinthian columns and a carved mantelpiece

Elegant swags and jabots enhance the windows in the comfortably furnished parlor during the Wagner years.

rescued from the Bayard Mansion on State Street opposite the Bowery, close to one of Archibald Gracie's most elegant downtown homes. Off the ballroom were two smaller reception rooms. A short flight below were offices for the mayor and a secretary, a conference room, storage and coat rooms, and, at the request of City Hall reporters, a press room.

Mrs. Francis Henry Lenygon, an interior decorator who had worked on the White House and Blair House restorations, furnished the rooms with Hepplewhite, Adam, Sheraton, and Sheffield pieces on loan from the customary museums as well as antiques and reproduction pieces donated by private citizens. These architectural and deco-

rative efforts provided an aesthetic connection with the main house.

As for a physical connection with the main house, there was none. Mrs. Wagner hadn't *wanted* one. Her intention was to keep home and wing apart. As a result, guests would, for the next twenty years, be forced to pass through the family quarters or out of one building and into the other.

The Susan E. Wagner memorial wing opened on September 27, 1966. Finally, Ada Louise Huxtable of the *Times* was impressed, calling the neoclassical work an "impeccably executed, superbly appointed addition to Gracie Mansion."

Architect Mott B. Schmidt's rendering for the eighteenth-century-style reception wing proposed by Susan Wagner as the solution to too many visitors wandering through the mansion. In submitting his 1965 design to the Art Commission of the City of New York, Schmidt provides an estimate of $500,000. When completed in 1966, the beautifully furnished addition will have cost $800,000, all of it contributed by private citizens.

Still grieving, Mayor Robert Wagner takes part in the May 1965 groundbreaking ceremony for the new wing that will be named in memory of his wife. (Jack I. Poses, chairman of the project's executive committee, stands by.) "We do not need ceremonial shovels, but will you please have three ordinary shovels or spades on the premises," Parks Commissioner Newbold Morris advised his chief engineer in a memo admirably down-to-earth.

A luncheon in the ballroom on January 15, 1984, for Zhao Ziyang, the premier of China. Other international leaders at the many receptions and feasts in the Koch years would include Jacques Chirac, then the mayor of Paris, and Hosni Mubarak, the president of Egypt.

After the ball is over. Mott Schmidt based his ballroom design on that of "The Vale," the splendid Theodore Lyman House in Waltham, Massachusetts, built about 1790.

Mark Hampton's unrealized proposal
for the ballroom's decorative scheme.

Hampton's handsome installation of a drawing room in the Wagner Wing features a mahogany center table attributed to Joseph Meeks c. 1840 that was donated to the mansion by a member of the Gracie family. Walls of Titian red create a cozy room frequently used for small dinners during the Koch administration.

How to perk things up? "I'd paint the walls yellow and put red carpets on the floors," Mrs. Lindsay's decorator briskly advised. And so she did, in the entrance hall, library, and parlor (above).

"I think it just rotted," said Mary Lindsay, who discovered the torn curtain in the parlor on a tour before moving in. Too much wear-and-tear, too little respect. "It just broke my heart."

AFTER HER HUSBAND'S ELECTION in 1965, Mrs. John Lindsay brought a consultant, Mrs. John Pemberton, in for a look. Mrs. Pemberton, an old family friend, was a decorator of no-nonsense style.

"What would you do with this house?" the first lady asked.

"I'd paint the walls yellow and put red carpets on the floors," the second replied.

"And that's exactly what we did," Mrs. Lindsay recalled. The living room was painted yellow, the library was painted yellow, and so was the front hall—which contained the grandfather clock from LaGuardia's day and the scroll-armed mahogany sofa from Noah Wheaton's. A red broadloom carpet covered the oak floor and ran up the grand staircase. The bedrooms were done in pastels. "We tried to make it as simple and unornate as possible, since it is an old country farmhouse, after all. We just painted it, basically.

"The guys had to scrape off layers and layers of paint from those beautiful old mantelpieces, because apparently in the years previous they'd just painted over everything instead of bothering to get back to the bare wood and start again the right way. It was a lot of work. We also had to replace a lot of the posts on the staircase. They'd just gotten tired. The house had had a lot of hard usage. Three or four groups were walking through every day. There were tables—museum pieces!—that had been ruined when people poured water into plants without using saucers. It was terrible." So the Lindsays brought along most of their own furniture and china—including the dining table and chairs that had belonged to the mayor's father.

For the Parks Department, practicality remained the priority. The torn was mended, the broken replaced. Regarding the incoming mayor's quarters: "This room in its present state lacks a great deal of furniture in order to make it liveable. The rug needs cleaning and some attention should be given to the fluorescent [sic] which appears to be exuding from behind the tiles in the walls of the shower room," were among the many observations in a three-page interoffice memorandum written in November 1965, by Samuel M. White, the Director of Maintenance and Operation.

The Beames' library focused on the TV. Reproduction furniture and celadon walls are typical of the 1970s taste for painterly abstract floral prints.

Outside, the same. The pilasters and decking on the porch received some needed attention, and the reed-and-rattan furniture was worn out. It had been purchased during the Impellitteri administration.

"THIS HOUSE WILL REFLECT MRS. BEAME," announced interior decorator Joan Haber in 1974 as she bent to the task for which the city had allotted $40,000. "We will keep things warm and perfumy the way she is."

Early rumors had swirled about a palette of mushroom, mustard, and eggplant, but the new first lady went lighter and brighter. The living room walls were covered in pale green water-silk paper, the library and dining room in cream, and the bedrooms in more fussy prints—one in a yellow floral with tulips, another in a red pattern with matching bedspreads and curtains. The breakfast room was dolled up in lime green and white, and the mayor's study in Wedgwood blue to match his eyes.

The State Bedroom's sprightly yellow-ground walls are the backdrop for a piece of the nineteenth-century faux bamboo furniture juxtaposed with a small refrigerator.

The breakfast room is enveloped in a frond-patterned covering on the ceiling and walls, creating a gardenlike setting.

Nathaniel Prime Mansion, Hell Gate near Yorkville, N.Y., watercolor, gouache, and graphite on paper, by William Rickarby Miller, 1854. The soft ochre-yellow exterior of this lovely riverside estate, built to the northwest of Gracie's around the same time as his, represents the popular pastel scheme of that time and place. "We were very influenced by the rendering," says architect Charles A. Platt, so during the Koch and Bloomberg restorations Gracie Mansion was painted the same ochre yellow.

GUIDED BY HENRY GELDZAHLER, his commissioner of cultural affairs, Ed Koch borrowed modern works from important museums and galleries—works by John Marin, Emil Nolde, Al Held, Alex Katz, Larry Rivers, Hans Hofmann, Jules Olitski, Richard Hennessy, and others. Most whimsical of the batch was "Pee Wee," Anne Arnold's black-and-white rabbit sculpted of polyester resin and wood, which moved into the mayor's bedroom with him. But Gracie Mansion needed a lot more than cosmetic adornment.

With the spirited efforts of Joan K. Davidson, a preservationist and president of the J. M. Kaplan Fund, Koch agreed to a complete overhaul. In 1981, he established the Gracie Mansion Conservancy to preserve, maintain, and enhance New York's most important house—and, as its first assignment, to oversee a $5.5-million renovation. "The mayor wanted all the money to be raised privately," says Diane Mulcahy Coffey, Koch's chief of staff, who led the fund-raising effort, "with the city having responsibility for maintaining the house. So the city gave $1 million, and we raised the other $4.5."

Detail of a corner section of the mantel in an upstairs bedroom, photographed for the Historic American Buildings Survey in August 1984, during the Koch restoration.

"The house was falling apart, literally," Ed Koch says today. "It was in terrible shape. Nothing had been done for many, many years." And so the work began, in March 1983.

The mayor also insisted that the mansion be a public treasure. "The guiding principle was the White House principle," explains Mrs. Davidson, who was named the Conservancy's chairman: "To have an institutional framework that remains constant and to maintain the house as a public responsibility. Mayors come and go, politics change, but the basic structure remains. We felt that New York should have no less."

Given the go-ahead, she gathered architects and archaeologists, artisans, and curators to share their expertise. Charles A. Platt—the New York architect whose grandfather, Charles Adams Platt (1861–1933), had been an architect and landscape artist—became the coordinating architect, and preservationist Robert Meadows, who had worked on Hamilton Grange, Old Westbury, and Fraunces Tavern, was named the architect of record. The main house and wing would be decorated by two of New York's most exalted practitioners: Albert Hadley, who had worked on homes for Whitneys, Rockefellers, and Paleys

"The overhang above the porch could very well have fallen if the pillars hadn't been strengthened," the mayor says. In rebuilding the porch, the basement was extended to provide more space for offices, storage, staff, and security.

in his longtime partnership with Mrs. Henry Parish, and Mark Hampton, who had recently done the Naval Observatory in Washington for Vice President George Bush. "We're trying for authenticity without pulling the wool over anyone's eyes," Hampton told *House Beautiful*. "The decorating has to be flexible enough so the carpet can be rolled up for press conferences, the furniture rearranged for ceremonial dinners." Deborah Krulewitch, the Conservancy's executive director, would be "clerk of the works," according to Joan Davidson, "the one to hold all the strands together."

In March 1983, the structural work began—and the archaeological digs. When the basement was enlarged for staff quarters and storage space, and the rotting porch was rebuilt, Gracie Mansion yielded wonderful finds.

Among them: a small cannonball, assumed to be a relic of the skirmish fought at Jacob Walton's house during the American Revolution. Other shovels unearthed remnants of

an eighteenth-century sewage system, clay pipes, wine bottles and chinaware, sandstone columns that supported the original porch, and a beehive oven in the basement that would have been part of Walton's house.

"When Gracie bought the Walton house, we believe it was facing south, and the archaeologists found what might have been a cobblestone drive," says Meadows, who is now assistant vice president for facilities and university architect at the University of Indiana.

"There are many mysteries about that house," says Dianne Pilgrim, who was the curator of decorative arts at the Brooklyn Museum when she joined the working committee as a founding member of the Conservancy. "The parlor is very odd, for instance. Nothing's centered. The fireplace, the lighting fixture—everything's off. And the door leading into the kitchen: That's odd. There's a lot nobody knows."

In order to uncover the mansion's original paint colors,

LEFT: An archaeologist digging in the basement under the front hall unearths a piece of Chinese export ware that might have come from a Gracie or Walton cupboard.

RIGHT: This small cannonball from the Revolutionary War is another gritty relic found during the excavation. Was it a culprit in the attack on Jacob Walton's home?

Platt says they did "more than one hundred biopsies, or penetrations, behind the shutters and next to frames and things."

"The house was tampered with many, many times by different owners," adds Meadows. "The majority of the finishes had been stripped, and the places we found were in newer-hung ceilings or had been covered over when they put the elevator in." The team removed paint with scalpels. Every chip was embedded in acrylic, then cut at an angle, and examined under a microscope—which revealed such subtleties as dirt between the layers. "If you're lucky," he says, "you can get a chronology."

For as long as anyone could remember, the exterior had been painted a cold white with black or dark green shutters, which reminded Platt of a suburban funeral home or country club. Now, research revealed that the palette of 1810 had been a soft ocher yellow with white trim and ivy-green shutters. Such a pastel palette had been popular in this summer colony, and with confirmation from a watercolor of the Nathaniel Prime house, an estate near Gracie's in the early 1800s wearing the very same colors, the exterior could be dressed in its authentic coat.

Infrared scanning helped determine the original framing. The architects wanted to know how the floors met the walls, which would reveal the original layout of rooms, if possible. This required raising the temperature to over 100 degrees and it was already summer.

"Ed was a great sport, and he never complained," says Meadows. "We got him out for a while and cranked up the boiler for about twelve hours. There were window air-conditioners in each room, which we then turned on full blast to maximum cool. After a couple of hours, when we'd lost the heat and gotten the temperature back to normal, we could 'read' the structure of the house. We knew that the historic portion had nogging in the walls—a combination of

OPPOSITE: "My idea was exactly what Mrs. Parish and Jackie Kennedy did at the White House," says Albert Hadley of his designs for Gracie Mansion. "Make it up to date and liveable without making it a museum." This charming rendering shows his unrealized scheme for the library, using classic Parish-Hadley striped upholstered furniture with a dramatic nineteenth-century Colza chandelier.

low-fired brick held together with mortar of straw, clay, and a little lime that dates back to medieval times. The mass of the masonry and the supporting wood frame lose their heat at a different rate, so we were running around with an infrared camera looking at different walls. The resulting image in this test looks like an X-ray of the human body, so we could really see how the house was put together. The sad part was that we couldn't record it. We had no device to."

FROM THE START, the interior operation was beset by questions of authority and authenticity. "Everyone had an opinion," says Mrs. Davidson. "It was not easy."

In reality, purism was not always feasible. For a museum, strict allegiance to nineteenth-century styles and materials might apply. As a home for living mayors and their families, however, the mansion would have to include modern conveniences, lead-free paint, and comfortable furniture.

"I set about this thing the way I'd done on my jobs in the past and made my sketches," says Albert Hadley, the distinguished interior designer, in his black turtleneck sweater and Nashville accent. "I wanted to make the house true to its aesthetic and its period, but I felt it should be a house of today that has grown *out* of the past." In the mayor's bedroom, Hadley replaced Koch's modern Swedish bed from Greenwich Village with a new one of elegant simplicity. In came a Federal linen press, and the polyester rabbit stayed in place.

Hadley had acquired a real treasure: a valuable wall covering—"Les Jardins de Paris" by Zuber—that had been found, unused and in its original wrapping, in the attic of a Hudson Valley house. This scenic masterpiece, printed with hand-carved, pear-wood blocks in 1830, didn't fit the front hall but was just right for the dining room. To complement it, the decorator ordered simple muslin curtains and a rug with a moiré pattern in shades of green.

Function over form was a continuous problem. Take the library. "To tell you the truth, no one knew what to do with it," says Dianne Pilgrim, who is now director emeritus and senior advisor for special projects at the Cooper-Hewitt National Design Museum. "Koch used it a lot, and there was all this electronic stuff—a TV, music equipment. He really loved to bring in people he worked with downtown, and they'd put their feet up on the table. We knew we couldn't be too historically correct in that room, because it would be destroyed." Hadley chose a rich, varnished green for the walls and commissioned a rug to be woven in wavy stripes.

The next thing he knew, the floor coverings had been switched. "The striped rug looked beautiful in the dining room," says Davidson, but Hadley felt otherwise. With the rugs pulled out from under him, he left the project.

His schemes for the other rooms were dropped, and the job was completed by Marilynn Johnson, who had been an associate curator of the American wing at the Metropolitan Museum of Art, and her associate, Lisa Krieger—both specialists in the Federal period. For the State Bedroom, they selected a furniture set of faux bamboo from the late nineteenth century. For the parlor, which Hadley had envisioned in yellows, sepias, and tobacco brown, they chose a documented blue-and-ocher wallpaper and an Empire Napoleon carpet featuring rosettes within squares. Even then, Johnson had her doubts about the competing motifs, but too late; the deadline was nigh. "Pattern with pattern can be okay, but I wasn't really happy with that combination," she admits now.

The front hall became a veritable field of combat, especially regarding the painted floor. Such ornamentation had been popular in the summer houses of Gracie's day. Investigation evokes a *Rashomon*-like saga concerning attribution and derivation, floor cloth versus whole floor, but it seems certain that it was Lisa Krieger's research—and color scheme

Hadley's proposed design for the dining room, with a moiré-patterned carpet in shades of green.

OPPOSITE: The completed dining room showcases the Zuber scenic wall covering with a light ochre wainscot and 1920s cut-glass chandelier. The rest of the furnishings are still on view in this room, except for the controversial striped carpet.

of ochre and charcoal—that won the debate. Decorative artist Stephen Gemberling painted a faux-marble diamond pattern similar to what might have been there in 1810, with a central medallion and a compass inspired by (depending on the source) either a piece of scrimshaw or the trade card of a nineteenth-century artisan who painted such floors. Gemberling also marbleized the baseboards and the stairs.

"We all loved it," says Davidson. Well, not quite all. "The medallion was okay," Hadley allows, "but I considered it a mistake to carry the marbling up the stairs. The Gracies never would have done that."

The kitchen, which was the domain of Mayor Koch's chef, Mitchel London, became the focus of too many cooks. "You had a single mayor who worked very, very hard and came home late, and Mitchel, who had Ed's ear. And what Mitchel wanted was an industrial kitchen," says Meadows. "So we designed two kitchens—a residential kitchen, and a commer-

cial kitchen. I'd bought the refrigerator and stove—they were *there*—but the residential kitchen was ripped out, and the commercial kitchen enlarged. We also had a kosher kitchen done for Ed, which was really nothing more than a pantry with a sink."

One of the greatest accomplishments of all was the architectural hyphen inserted between the house and wing. "The working committee decided very early that a proper connection had to be attained somehow," says Platt, and the two architects made it happen. No longer would popes and poets have to troop through the kitchen or basement enroute to the ballroom.

But in order to build the connection, the stairway in the entrance hall would have to undergo major surgery. "There was a lot of discussion," says Meadows, "and we concluded that it would be best to reconfigure it. It wasn't self-supporting. There was a wall going straight down under it, because

there were bathrooms there. When we opened it up, we made the stairway freestanding and gave it a more graceful turn."

In the Wagner Wing, Mark Hampton was out-voted several times, one involving his desire to place two large pieces of sculpture or two large busts in the niches at either end of the ballroom. "I really respected his talent, and *he* had a respect for history," says Marilynn Johnson.

In her quest to return the interior to its glory days (or as close to them as possible, given contemporary conditions), Joan Davidson asked John Dobkin, then director of the

National Academy of Design, to gather furnishings from every period of New York history. "My effort was to get my museum buddies to lend paintings and decorative arts," he recalls. "We didn't have any one painting or piece of furniture in mind. We just wanted to get the best things we could. The ensemble made all the sense in the world and showed off the house to its best advantage. The place looked wonderful."

The mayor opened the doors to the press in November 1984. "I don't think that this house will have to be restored again for another two hundred years," he said with pride.

The parlor in 1986 is a patterned confection of historical correctness. The chandelier, painting, sconces, center table, and card tables are at home in the room to this day.

*Mayor, Mayor,
how does your
garden grow?*

IN THE GRACIE YEARS, the grounds were embellished by gardens, a greenhouse, and possibly an orchard. In the LaGuardia years, four cabbages were planted by the mayor's daughter. In the Lindsay years, new landscape designs were drawn up by the mayor's mother-in-law.

But Ed Koch wanted more. The renovation of the house, paths, and parking area were nearly complete, and it was time to consider the rest. The archaeological digs and construction had torn up almost every living thing; only boxwood, ferns, and a yew hedge remained.

Koch was unhappy with a palette so green. So in 1987, Maureen Hackett, a young horticulturist who had worked on the Conservatory Garden in Central Park, arrived to provide him with a paradise of color.

Flanking the porch steps at the main entrance, she designed a border of blue and white salvia, ageratum, buddleia, cleome, santolina, nicotiana, veronica, tulips, and various types of petunia—"informal," she says, "like a cottage garden." In a bed of crabapple trees near the fence, she planted red, yellow, and orange tulips, and on the lawn, carved a serpentine bed for a crowd of daffodils, begonias, and impatiens. On the northeastern perimeter, she planted forty feet of roses, experimenting with *Alberic Barbier*, *Queen Elizabeth*, *Nearly Wild*, *Peace*, and French climbers. And off the Wagner Wing terrace, she planted an enclosed white garden, which showed up beautifully in the evening after a party in the ballroom.

For Mitchel London, the executive chef, she planted an herb garden with sage, rosemary, tarragon, dill, and parsley—some of which she herself used to keep bugs off the roses (although she couldn't save the begonias from the pigeons).

Hackett lived nearby and was on the job full-time, with an office in the basement, and the company of her dog, Cody. "He had the run of the house," she says, "and he was spoiled rotten, with all those wonderful scraps and big lamb bones from the receptions. Ed Koch would sometimes meet people in the green library, with Cody curled up at his feet."

She herself met people all over the place—Jesse Jackson

in the kitchen, movie director John Boorman on the lawn, and Robert F. Wagner Jr., then president of the board of education, when he wandered outside after a meeting.

"I just wanted to tell you I grew up here," Bobby Wagner told her. "And it's never looked more beautiful."

From her cutting garden on the northeastern perimeter, Hackett fashioned bouquets for the ballroom and parlor; more lavish arrangements came from outside florists. "It was like living on this great estate," she says. "The mayor loved all that. He entertained a lot."

When she wasn't clipping and snipping, Hackett was often sent shopping. "I was technically the horticulturist," she says, "but I'd go out to get cakes or something when Mitchel needed them. We all did everything. It was like a family affair."

Only one thing raised her hackles: when guests tossed their ice cubes into the flower beds.

But that's a perennial problem.

The "cottage garden" before (opposite) and
after the ministrations of Maureen Hackett.

IN THE EARLY DAYS OF GIULIANI, the mansion underwent another sprucing up. The exterior was repainted and the chimneys stripped to their original brick. More antiques were elicited from museums and the private sector, and decorator Albert Hadley was invited to return.

"I went through the same spiel with them as far as making it a comfortable house and respecting the history," he says today. "I freshened up the dining room, and they couldn't have been more agreeable. But we needed money for good furniture—especially in the parlor, which had never been properly furnished—and we couldn't do very much."

In the library, Caroline Giuliani added her name to Millie's window, with the help of a glazier.

Jamie Drake, on the job. His initial proposal for the Bloomberg parlor is seen in this watercolor elevation (above). The plum color scheme was hotly debated between Conservancy members and the designer, resulting in the final choice of patent yellow and moss green.

OFFICIALLY, HE WAS AN ANONYMOUS DONOR, but everyone knew that it was Mayor Michael R. Bloomberg himself who was contributing $5 million toward the restoration of the home he was not even calling his own. The mayor had decided to stay in his five-story Beaux Arts limestone townhouse and to use Gracie Mansion for city functions and eminent overnight guests.

Jamie Drake, who had decorated the mayor's townhouse as well as his other houses, was known for gracious flair and vivid color. "People don't come to me for beige or for Laura Ashley sweet," he had previously informed *Elle Décor* magazine. "I have very bold taste." But while his hues and cry stirred the traditionalists, they didn't faze the mayor or the Gracie Mansion Conservancy, whose mission it would be to approve the overall concepts and color schemes.

"The house has wonderful bones," Drake said as he rolled up his elegant sleeves in the winter of 2002. "A great classical center-hall layout, with four major rooms downstairs and

OPPOSITE: Bloomberg in the ballroom.

The dining room under wraps, summer of 2002.

five major rooms upstairs. The proportions of the rooms are gracious if not grand, with wonderful symmetries, and they're flooded with light.

"This was originally a country seat, but it might well have had fancy furniture and chandeliers. So we're keeping to the 1810 period and going with grander stuff—and as much New York furniture as possible. Some walls will be painted, some papered, with lots of faux finishes."

And lots of color. Out with the soft and murky; in with the brilliant and brave! "What we think of as muted 'Williamsburg' tones are actually colors that have deteriorated through decades of smoke and light. As color-analysis technology has improved, it's been discovered that the colors of previous centuries were brighter than anyone imagined," Drake explained, citing the vibrant shades used in such other American country seats as Monticello and Mount Vernon.

What no one could cite in any of this was the taste of Archibald Gracie. What were *his* colors? What was *his* taste?

"When the house was built, how did he conceive of it?" mused Dianne Pilgrim, who'd played a major role in the Koch restoration. "Did he consider it grand? Did he consider it just a summer escape? You have so little to go on."

When structural work began, the original nogging in the exterior walls was deemed to be still effective, so it was left in place. But many moldings, windows, and chair railings were deteriorating, so craftsmen filled cracks and grooved out portions that had rotted or shifted over the years.

The week before painting was to start, the staircase became structurally unstable. "It was starting to fall away from the wall," says Joel Arencibia, the project manager for Crocker Construction Ltd. "Heavy stuff was being carried upstairs, and we noticed the spindles were off at a slight angle."

"The structure was *beyond* compromised, to the point of being dangerous," adds decorator Drake, who, like preservationist Robert Meadows of the Koch restoration, believes the staircase was installed in the 1920s and has probably been

redone, moved, and enlarged several times since. On this occasion, it was reinforced with steel supports.

So many ups and downs, so little time! When plumbers turned off the water before tackling the bathrooms, they discovered the mansion had only *one* turn-off valve (most houses have one in every bathroom), and its threading was so corroded they couldn't turn the water back on. "We had to go into the main water supply on East End Avenue, which required permission to shut off all of East End Avenue for four hours," says Drake.

The library, which was originally the largest room in Archibald Gracie's house and is nearly every mayor's favorite, has been sponge-glazed in French blue. The parlor walls have been painted "patent yellow," a color that was popular in similar homes of the early nineteenth century, with faux marble on the green wainscoting to camouflage wear and tear. This is the fancy-dress room, and to honor it, Drake went to Scalamandré, the esteemed American firm, which has been designing and creating silk fabrics and trimmings for over seventy years. Famous for its decorative contributions to the White House, Blair House, Monticello, Hyde Park, the United States Capitol, and Mount Vernon, this was the proper source for the mansion. To dress the three double-hung windows, Drake wanted "Federal Stripe" drapes like those made for the Kennedys. But Bristol blue-and-gold is a combination exclusive to the White House, so he and the Conservancy created a special palette of moss green and patent yellow.

In the foyer, the striped wallpaper and painted floor echo the renovations of 1984, which recreated early nineteenth- century wall and floor treatments. Painted anew by five craftsmen from the Alpha Workshops—a New York design and decorative-painting studio that trains and employs artists living with HIV—the project took nine days. "It was meant to look faux, but intentionally naïve," says Ken Wampler, Alpha's executive director. Drake wanted it to look as if it had been done by itinerant painters at the end of the nineteenth century.

"We had a fifteen-week planning-and-prep phase and then fifteen weeks for all the construction, plumbing, electricity, painting, and installing the furnishings," Drake says.

RIGHT: A section of marble mosaic floor, newly installed in one of the bathrooms and partially covered by builder's protection.

The restoration, the total cost of which was $7 million, was to be finished by September 11, 2002, the one-year anniversary of the World Trade Center attacks, as a sign of New York City's resilience and ability to rebuild. And so it was, in a miraculous fifteen weeks. Michael Bloomberg, like Archibald Gracie before him, is a man who gets things done.

THROUGH MERCHANTS AND MAYORS, winters and springs, as the city soars and the backyard shrinks, Gracie Mansion endures. More than a dignified survivor in a city that persists in tearing itself down, more than a genteel dowager dusted with history, it has become—like the White House, Mount Vernon, 10 Downing Street—an iconic address. Whether New York's chief executive chooses to keep his pipe and pajamas here or to host only the occasional enchanted evening, this graceful place is the mayor's house.

And ours.

The restoration moves along speedily, stroke by stroke and rung by rung.

Louise Bourgeois's
Quarantania, III.
1949–50. Bronze, cast
2001. One of five
sculptures on loan to
Gracie Mansion from
the collection of the
Museum of Modern Art.

OPPOSITE: From the
inside out

This Egyptian Revival pier table on the parlor's east wall belonged to the Gracies. Veneered in mahogany with a marble top, gilt bronze mounts, painted legs, and a mirrored back, it was the height of fashion in 1815 New York.

"The brilliant patent yellow of the parlor is typically early nineteenth-century, when its vibrancy amplified light in a time before electricity," says Drake. The sumptuous valances are trimmed in silk-wrapped wood-mold fringe, a trimming so intricate that New York's house of Scalamandré devotes 1,000 hours to producing one yard. The Federal stripe of the curtains was custom-woven in New York, and the wallpaper border was custom-printed, based on a document from the Nancy McClelland Historic Wallpapers archive. The carpet design dates from 1827. Furnishings include pieces attributed to Duncan Phyfe and other notable New York cabinetmakers. The marble mantelpiece, purchased in France in the 1820s, is the only addition Joseph Foulke made to the house when he lived here.

OPPOSITE: The dining room's existing décor was enhanced with the addition of a new carpet installed during the Giuliani years. Drake added the period bronze-and-gilt-bronze chandelier.

FOLLOWING PAGE: "Les Jardins de Paris," Zuber's exquisite masterpiece, up close.

The foyer presents a legacy from the Wheaton years. This late classical scroll-armed mahogany sofa was made in New York around 1850 and came back to the house in 1966 as a gift from Noah Wheaton's descendants.

OPPOSITE: The splendid Empire buffet in the dining room, attributed to Lannuier, is one of the jewels in the collection and may have been used in one of the Gracies' downtown homes. It was donated to the mansion by Thomas J. Higginson, a Gracie descendant. Mirrored back panels and columnar legs add to its sophisticated character.

The library's French blue palette is a handsome backdrop for the portrait of William Gracie, first son of the house (above). The fine neo-classic sofa and marble-topped library table are attributed to Duncan Phyfe, and the carpet, based on a period document, was custom-colored to coordinate

with the existing carpet in the adjoining dining room. The dentil crown molding dates from 1799, when this was the largest room in Gracie's mansion, but the ceiling's panel molding with arc'd corners was a late-nineteenth-century addition.

FOLLOWING PAGE: A long shot of the library.

The exuberant chinoiserie wallpaper in the State Sitting Room was hand-printed from the original 1835 blocks. Capacious tufted chairs sit on the antique Oushak carpet.

OPPOSITE: The second floor, previously off-limits to the public because it was private living quarters, is now on view. The State Bedroom, where Nelson Mandela stayed during the Dinkins administration, features a suite of faux bamboo furniture made in New York in the late nineteenth century. The Argand chandelier is French, circa 1820. The decorative scheme of sprigged wallpaper, patterned carpet, and chintz nods to this period in design.

Mott Schmidt's architecture in the ballroom has been enhanced by brilliant Wedgwood-blue walls of Venetian plaster (a time-honored concoction that uses cement, lime, linseed oil, and ground marble dust). The carved mantelpiece of the 1790s was salvaged from the Bayard Mansion at 7 State Street downtown.

OPPOSITE: Welcome to the Wagner Wing, and a staircase devised for grand entrances. "The Wing addresses all the needs of contemporary life and can host events for the hundreds," Drake says, "yet it's detailed in the neo-classic fashion." His selection of a rich blue-and-gold runner leads guests to the 1,000-square-foot ballroom. The faux stone-block walls are an homage to Mark Hampton's 1986 design.

The portrait of Susan E. Wagner by Willy Pogany resides in the sun-flooded corner drawing room of the reception wing she was so instrumental in creating. The pale apricot walls and cinnamon-toned fabrics add to its warmth.

OPPOSITE: One of the Wagner Wing's two drawing rooms, redone with rich cobalt-blue walls as a contrast to the mahogany furnishings. The elegant curtains are based on a design from a period pattern book. The bull's-eye mirror is the twin of the mirror in the mansion's dining room.

Acknowledgments

My profound appreciation to Jamie Drake, whose resplendent restoration of Gracie Mansion was the impetus for this book, and to Gail Eisen, who brought us together.

I am deeply grateful to the Gracie Mansion Conservancy and the Mayor's Office for their support. Thanks to Mary Beth Betts, Patti Harris, and Nanette Smith.

For their firsthand reports on first-family life there, I am delighted to thank Buddy Beame and his sons, Andrew and Richard; Mayor Ed Koch; the late Mary Lindsay and her grown-up children Katharine Lake, Dr. Anne Lindsay, John V. Lindsay, Jr., and Margi Picotte; and Duncan Wagner. And although Diane M. Coffey, Sid Frigand, Rozanne Gold, Maureen Hackett, Mitchel London, and Henry J. Stern weren't exactly members of the mayoral family, they might as well have been.

Access to historic files, reports, photos, and mayoral scrap-books was graciously provided by the Art Commssion of the City of New York, the Landmarks Preservation Commission, the Historic House Trust of New York City, the New York City Department of Parks and Recreation, and the New York City Municipal Archives.

I am indebted to Susan Olsen at the Woodlawn Cemetery for guiding me to Archibald Gracie's grave, to Norman Brouwer at the South Street Seaport Museum Library, and to Stuart Frank, Michael P. Dyer, and Michael Lapides at the New Bedford Whaling Museum for their deep-sea dives in pursuit of Gracie's fleet.

For sharing their colorful insights on the 1980s restoration, I am grateful to Libby Cameron, Joan K. Davidson, John Dobkin, Albert Hadley, Duane Hampton, Marilynn Johnson, Lisa Krieger, Robert E. Meadows, Paula Perlini, Dianne H. Pilgrim, and Charles A. Platt. And to those who

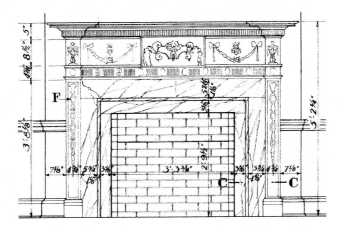

Detail of a bedroom fireplace from a record drawing of 1935.

so patiently explained their roles in the refurbishment of 2002: Connie Athas, Joel Arencibia, John A. Sacchetti Donis, Edward A. Goodman, Gordon Roth, Russell Van Peterson, and Ken Wampler.

A bouquet to the following friends, whose interest in this project enriched it significantly: Dr. Richard K. Lieberman and Douglas DiCarlo at the LaGuardia and Wagner Archives of LaGuardia Community College/CUNY; Marilyn Ibach and Amy Williams at the Library of Congress; Marguerite Lavin, Eileen Morales, and Angela Mattia at the Museum of the City of New York; Dr. Kenneth T. Jackson and Eleanor Gillers at the New-York Historical Society; Rupert Murdoch, Anne Aquilina, Paul Armstrong, and Laura A. Harris at the *New York Post;* and everyone at the New York Society Library.

Tender loving thanks to Margo Feiden for her exuberant generosity, Kenneth Cobb for his prodigious digs, Madeline Rogers for her well-tempered counsel, Katie Stern for the input and outtakes, and John Tauranac, elegant and essential. For their participation above and beyond, I thank Kathleen Jayes, my editor, and Holly Rothman, her valiant associate at Rizzoli, and Neeti Madan, my agent and champion.

And, finally, two curtseys to Alice Gore King and Isabella Hardy Watts, enchanting ladies and great-great-granddaughters of Archibald Gracie.

Bibliography

Albion, Robert Greenhalgh. *The Rise of New York Port*. New York: Charles Scribner's Sons, 1939.

Barrett, Walter. *The Old Merchants of New York City*. New York: Carleton, 1862 and 1863.

Black, Mary. *New York City's Gracie Mansion: A History of the Mayor's House*. New York: The J. M. Kaplan Fund for The Gracie Mansion Conservancy, 1984.

Bliven, Bruce Jr. *Under the Guns*. New York: Harper & Row, 1972.

Brookhiser, Richard. *Alexander Hamilton, American*. New York: The Free Press, 1999.

Brooks, Van Wyck. *The World of Washington Irving*. New York: E. P. Dutton & Company, Inc., 1944.

Brown, Henry Collins, editor. *Valentine's Manual of the City of New York for 1916–17* (New Series No. 1). New York: The Valentine Company, 1916.

———. *Valentine's Manual of Old New York 1922* (New Series No. 6). New York: Valentine's Manual Inc., 1921.

———. *Valentine's Manual of Old New York 1924*. Year Book of the Museum of the City of New York. New York: Gracie Mansion, 1923.

———. *Valentine's Manual of Old New York 1925*. Year Book of the Museum of the City of New York. New York: Gracie Mansion, 1924.

———. *Valentine's Manual of Old New York 1927*. Hastings-on-Hudson: Valentine's Manual Inc., 1926.

Caemmerer, H. Paul. *The Life of Pierre Charles L'Enfant*. New York: Da Capo Press, 1950, reprinted 1970.

Caro, Robert A. *The Power Broker*. New York: Alfred A. Knopf, 1974.

Cerf, Bennett. *At Random*. New York: Random House, 1977.

Comstock, Sarah. *Old Roads from the Heart of New York*. New York: G.P. Putnam's Sons, 1915.

Culbertson, Judi and Tom Randall. *Permanent New Yorkers*. Chelsea: Chelsea Green Publishing Company, 1987.

Cutler, Carl C. *Queens of the Western Ocean*. Annapolis: United States Naval Institute, 1961.

Delehanty, Randolph and Martin Van Jones. *Classic Natchez*. Savannah: Martin-St. Martin, 1996.

Ernst, Robert. *Rufus King*. Williamsburg: The University of North Carolina Press, 1968.

Fairburn, William Armstrong. *Merchant Sail*. Volume V. Center Lovell: Fairburn Marine Educational Foundation, Inc., 1945–1955.

Gebhard, Elizabeth L. *The Life and Ventures of the Original John Jacob Astor*. Hudson: Bryan Printing Co., 1915.

Gilder, Rodman. *The Battery*. Boston: Houghton Mifflin Company, 1936.

Giuliani, Rudolph W. *Leadership*. New York: Miramax Books/Hyperion, 2002.

Goldstone, Harmon H. and Martha Dalrymple. *History Preserved: A Guide to New York City Landmarks and Historic Districts*. New York: Simon and Schuster, 1974.

Gracie, Archibald. *The Truth About Chickamauga*. Boston: Houghton Mifflin Company, 1911.

———. *The Truth About the Titanic*. New York: Mitchell Kennerley, 1913.

Gracie, Constance Schack. *Personal Experiences in Life's Journey*. Washington: Chas. H. Potter & Co., Inc., 1919.

Hacker, Louis M. *Alexander Hamilton in the American Tradition*. New York: McGraw-Hill Book Company, Inc., 1957.

Hamburger, Philip. *Mayor Watching and Other Pleasures*. New York: Rinehart & Company, Inc., 1958.

Hayes, Helen and Anita Loos. *Twice Over Lightly*. New York: Harcourt Brace Jovanovich, Inc., 1972.

Heath, Major-General William. *Memoirs*. Boston: I. Thomas and E. T. Andrews, 1798 (reprinted New York: William Abbatt, 1901).

Hellman, George S., editor. *Letters of Washington Irving to Henry Brevoort*. New York: G. P. Putnam's Sons, 1918.

Hemstreet, Charles. *Nooks & Corners of Old New York*. New York: Charles Scribner's Sons, 1899.

Hendrickson, Robert. *Hamilton II*. New York: Mason/Charter, 1976.

Hentoff, Nat. *A Political Life: The Education of John V. Lindsay*. New York: Alfred A. Knopf, 1969.

Hewitt, Mark Alan. *The Architecture of Mott B. Schmidt*. New York: Rizzoli, 1991.

Huxtable, Ada Louise. *Classic New York*. Garden City: Anchor Books, 1964.

King, Charles R., editor. *The Life and Correspondence of Rufus King*. New York: G. P. Putnam's Sons, 1898.

Kleiger, Estelle Fox. The Trial of Levi Weeks. Chicago: Academy Chicago Publishers, 1989.

Koch, Edward I. *Citizen Koch*. New York: St. Martin's Press, 1992.

Kohl, Susan. *The Ghost of Gracie Mansion*. New York: Silver Moon Press, 1999.

Kouwenhoven, John A. *The Columbia Historical Portrait of New York*. New York: Icon Editions, Harper & Row, 1972.

Lamb, Martha J. *History of the City of New York*. New York: Valentine's Manual, Inc., 1921.

Lockwood, Sarah M. *New York—Not So Little and Not So Old*. Garden City: Doubleday, Page & Company, 1926.

McAdoo, Eva T. *How Do You Like New York?* New York: The Macmillan Company, 1936.

Manners, William. *Patience and Fortitude: Fiorello LaGuardia*. New York: Harcourt Brace Jovanovich, Inc., 1976.

Mitchell, Broadus. *Alexander Hamilton: The National Adventure 1788–1804*. New York: The Macmillan Company, 1962.

Mott, Hopper Striker. *The New York of Yesterday*. New York: G.P. Putnam's Sons, 1908.

O'Dwyer, William (Paul O'Dwyer, editor). *Beyond the Golden Door*. Jamaica: St. John's University, 1986.

Olshansky, Joan R., project director. *Gracie Mansion: A Historic Structures Report*. New York: The Landmarks Preservation Commission [n.d.].

A Picture of New-York in 1846. New York: Homans & Ellis, 1846.

Porter, Kenneth Wiggins. *John Jacob Astor*. Cambridge: Harvard University Press, 1931.

Restoring the Century-Old Residential Glories of the East River. New York: Henry Collins Brown, 1925.

Special Lists: List of American-Flag Merchant Vessels. Washington: The National Archives, General Services Administration, 1968.

Stokes, I. N. Phelps. *The Iconography of Manhattan Island*. New York: Arno Press Inc., 1967.

Syrett, Harold C., editor. *The Papers of Alexander Hamilton*. New York: Columbia University Press, 1977.

Tauranac, John. *Essential New York*. New York: Holt, Rinehart and Winston, 1979.

Van Rensselaer, Mrs. John King. *Hell Gate and Horen Hook*. New York, 1900.

Willensky, Elliot and Norval White. *AIA Guide to New York City*. San Diego: Harcourt Brace Jovanovich, 1988.

Worden, Helen. *Here Is New York*. New York: Doubleday, Doran & Company, Inc., 1939.

———. *Round Manhattan's Rim*. Indianapolis: The Bobbs-Merrill Company, 1934.

Illustration Credits

While every effort has been made to trace all present copyright holders of the material in this book, any unintentional omission is hereby apologized for in advance, and I would be pleased to correct any errors in acknowledgments in any future edition.

Page 1: The City of New York Department of Parks & Recreation, Capital Projects Division, Map File; *page 2:* The City of New York Department of Parks & Recreation, Capital Projects Division, Map File; *page 6:* The City of New York Department of Parks & Recreation, Capital Projects Division, Map File; *page 9:* The City of New York Department of Parks & Recreation, Capital Projects Division, Map File; *page 10:* The City of New York Department of Parks & Recreation, Capital Projects Division, Map File; *page 11:* The Library of Congress; *page 12:* Roger Goodspeed Family Collection; *page 13:* Spencer Collection, The New York Public Library; *page 14:* Spencer Collection, The New York Public Library; *page 15:* The Library of Congress; *page 16:* left, Courtesy of the New-York Historical Society, Gift of Mrs. Charles Jackson; middle top, Courtesy of the New-York Historical Society, Purchased from Mr. Frank Ganci; middle bottom, Courtesy of the New-York Historical Society, Gift of John Fiske in memory of his mother, Margaret Gracie Fiske; right, Courtesy of the Gracie Mansion Conservancy; *page 17:* left top, Courtesy of the New-York Historical Society; left bottom, Courtesy of the New-York Historical Society, Bequest of George Gibbs; right, Frick Art Reference Library; *page 18:* Author's collection; *page 19:* top, Courtesy of the Gracie Mansion Conservancy; bottom, the Library of Congress; *page 20: Valentine's Manual, 1864; page 21:* left, Courtesy of the New-York Historical Society; right, *Leslie's History of the Greater New York*, 1898; *page 22:* Courtesy of the New Bedford Whaling Museum © The New Bedford Whaling Museum; *page 23:* Eno Collection, The New York Public Library; *page 24:* The Library of Congress; *page 26:* © 2003 N.Y.P. Holdings Inc., D/B/A New York Post; *page 27: Valentine's Manual of Old New York, 1921; page 28:* Gift of Amelia R. Foulke © Museum of the City of New York; *page 29:* Courtesy of the New-York Historical Society; *page 30:* Courtesy of the New-York Historical Society; *page 31:* Author's collection; *page 32:* © Museum of the City of New York; *page 33:* Photograph by Brown Bros.

© Museum of the City of New York; *page 35:* Courtesy of the Gracie Mansion Conservancy; *page 36:* © Museum of the City of New York; *page 37:* © Museum of the City of New York; *page 38:* Cosmo Photo Service © Museum of the City of New York; *page 39:* New York City Parks Photo Archive; *page 40:* top, The Library of Congress; bottom, Alajos L. Schuszler/New York City Parks Photo Archive; *page 41:* top, P.G. Andrews/New York City Parks Photo Archive; bottom, Rodney McCay Morgan/New York City Parks Photo Archive; *page 43:* Illustration by Peter Stern; *page 44:* Author's collection; *page 45:* © 2003 N.Y.P. Holdings Inc., D/B/A New York Post; *page 46:* Courtesy of NYC Municipal Archives; *page 47:* Author's collection; *page 49:* The LaGuardia and Wagner Archives, LaGuardia Community College/The City University of New York; *page 50:* Courtesy of NYC Municipal Archives; *page 51:* © Al Hirschfeld. Art reproduced by special arrangement with Hirschfeld's exclusive representative, The Margo Feiden Galleries Ltd., New York. *www.alhirschfeld.com; page 52:* top, Courtesy of NYC Municipal Archives; bottom, Author's collection; *page 53:* top, Courtesy of NYC Municipal Archives; bottom, Alfred Eisenstadt/Time Life Pictures/Getty Images; *page 55:* Courtesy of NYC Municipal Archives; *page 56:* Courtesy of NYC Municipal Archives; *page 57:* Illustration by Peter Stern; *page 58:* left, Author's collection; right, © 2003 N.Y.P. Holdings Inc., D/B/A New York

Post; *page 59:* Courtesy of NYC Municipal Archives; *page 60:* © 2003 N.Y.P. Holdings Inc., D/B/A New York Post; *page 61:* © Al Hirschfeld. This image is from the drawing entitled *Mr. Tisch and The Mayors* from the collection of Mr. and Mrs. Preston Robert Tisch. Art reproduced by special arrangement with Hirschfeld's exclusive representative, The Margo Feiden Galleries Ltd., New York. *www.alhirschfeld.com; page 62:* © 2003 N.Y.P. Holdings Inc., D/B/A New York Post; *page 63:* Courtesy of NYC Municipal Archives; *page 64:* top, The LaGuardia and Wagner Archives, LaGuardia Community College/The City University of New York; bottom, Courtesy of NYC Municipal Archives; *page 65:* top, The LaGuardia and Wagner Archives, LaGuardia Community College/The City University of New York; bottom, Author's collection; *page 67:* © Al Hirschfeld. This image is from the drawing entitled *Mr. Tisch and The Mayors* from the collection of Mr. and Mrs. Preston Robert Tisch. Art reproduced by special arrangement with Hirschfeld's exclusive representative, The Margo Feiden Galleries Ltd., New York. *www.alhirschfeld.com; page 68:* left, © 2003 N.Y.P. Holdings Inc., D/B/A New York Post; right, John Dominis/Time Life Pictures/Getty Images; *page 69:* © 2003 N.Y.P. Holdings Inc., D/B/A New York Post; *page 70:* © 2003 N.Y.P. Holdings Inc., D/B/A New York Post; *page 71:* John Dominis/Time Life Pictures/Getty Images; *page 73:* Courtesy of NYC Municipal

Archives; *page 74:* © Al Hirschfeld. This image is from the drawing entitled *Mr. Tisch and The Mayors* from the collection of Mr. and Mrs. Preston Robert Tisch. Art reproduced by special arrangement with Hirschfeld's exclusive representative, The Margo Feiden Galleries Ltd., New York. *www.alhirschfeld.com*; *page 75:* © 2003 N.Y.P. Holdings Inc., D/B/A New York Post; *page 76:* Courtesy of the Gracie Mansion Conservancy; *page 77:* © 2003 N.Y.P. Holdings Inc., D/B/A New York Post; *page 78:* top, © 2003 N.Y.P. Holdings Inc., D/B/A New York Post; bottom, Courtesy of Sid Frigand; *page 79:* © Al Hirschfeld. This image is from the drawing entitled *Mr. Tisch and The Mayors* from the collection of Mr. and Mrs. Preston Robert Tisch. Art reproduced by special arrangement with Hirschfeld's exclusive representative, The Margo Feiden Galleries Ltd., New York. *www.alhirschfeld.com*; *page 80:* © 2003 N.Y.P. Holdings Inc., D/B/A New York Post; *page 81:* © 2003 N.Y.P. Holdings Inc., D/B/A New York Post; *page 82:* left top, Courtesy of Sid Frigand; right and bottom, Courtesy of NYC Municipal Archives; *page 84:* © 2003 N.Y.P. Holdings Inc., D/B/A New York Post; *page 85:* © Al Hirschfeld. This image is from the drawing entitled *Mr. Tisch and The Mayors* from the collection of Mr. and Mrs. Preston Robert Tisch. Art reproduced by special arrangement with Hirschfeld's exclusive representative, The Margo Feiden Galleries Ltd., New York. *www.alhirschfeld.com*; *page 86:* © 2003 N.Y.P. Holdings Inc.,

D/B/A New York Post; *page 87:* left, Courtesy of NYC Municipal Archives; right: © 2003 N.Y.P. Holdings Inc., D/B/A New York Post; *page 88:* Courtesy of NYC Municipal Archives; *page 89:* © Al Hirschfeld. This image is from the drawing entitled *Mr. Tisch and The Mayors* from the collection of Mr. and Mrs. Preston Robert Tisch. Art reproduced by special arrangement with Hirschfeld's exclusive representative, The Margo Feiden Galleries Ltd., New York. *www.alhirschfeld.com*; *page 90:* Courtesy of NYC Municipal Archives; *page 91:* © 2003 N.Y.P. Holdings Inc., D/B/A New York Post; *page 92:* top, Courtesy of NYC Municipal Archives; left bottom: William Abranowicz/A+C Anthology; right bottom, © 2003 N.Y.P. Holdings Inc., D/B/A New York Post; *page 93:* Photograph by Brigitte Stelzer; *page 94:* © Al Hirschfeld. This image is from the drawing entitled *Mr. Tisch and The Mayors* from the collection of Mr. and Mrs. Preston Robert Tisch. Art reproduced by special arrangement with Hirschfeld's exclusive representative, The Margo Feiden Galleries Ltd., New York. *www.alhirschfeld.com*; *page 95:* Office of the Mayor, Photo Unit, City of New York; *page 96:* left, The LaGuardia and Wagner Archives, LaGuardia Community College/The City University of New York; right, © 2003 N.Y.P. Holdings Inc., D/B/A New York Post; *page 97:* top, © 2003 N.Y.P. Holdings Inc., D/B/A New York Post; bottom, Courtesy of NYC Municipal Archives; *page 98:* top, Courtesy of the

New-York Historical Society; bottom, Courtesy of NYC Municipal Archives; *page 99:* left top, right top, right bottom, © 2003 N.Y.P. Holdings Inc., D/B/A New York Post; left bottom, Courtesy Maureen Hackett; *page 100:* Author's collection; *page 101:* The LaGuardia and Wagner Archives, LaGuardia Community College/The City University of New York; *page 102:* top, © 2003 N.Y.P. Holdings Inc., D/B/A New York Post; bottom, The LaGuardia and Wagner Archives, LaGuardia Community College/The City University of New York; *page 103:* top, Courtesy of NYC Municipal Archives; bottom, © 2003 N.Y.P. Holdings Inc., D/B/A New York Post; *page 104:* left top, © 2003 N.Y.P. Holdings Inc., D/B/A New York Post; right top, Courtesy of NYC Municipal Archives; left bottom, Author's collection; right bottom, Office of The Mayor, Photo Unit, City of New York; *page 105:* left top, Printed with the permission of Lord & Taylor, a division of the May Department Stores Company; left middle, Dances Patrelle's *The Yorkville Nutcracker,* photograph by Rosalie O'Connor; left bottom, Office of the Mayor, Photo Unit, City of New York, courtesy of *The Apprentice,* NBC Universal; right top, Author's collection; right bottom, Courtesy of Rocky H. Aoki; *page 106:* top, *The Ghost of Gracie Mansion* by Susan Kohl © 2000 Silver Moon Press. Illustration reprinted by permission of Ned Butterfield and Silver Moon Press; bottom, Photograph by Craig Blankenhorn © 2002 ABC

Photography Archives; *page 107:* Courtesy WPIX-TV, New York; *page 109:* Courtesy of the New-York Historical Society; *page 110:* left, Courtesy of the New-York Historical Society; right, Drake Design Associates. Photographs by William Waldron; *page 111:* The Library of Congress; *page 112:* Courtesy of the New-York Historical Society; *page 113:* Author's collection; *page 114:* Courtesy of the New-York Historical Society, Purchased from Rudolph F. Bunner; *page 115:* Courtesy of the New-York Historical Society, Gift of George A. Zabriskie; *page 116:* top, Courtesy of the New-York Historical Society; bottom, The Byron Collection © Museum of the City of New York; *page 117:* top, Courtesy of NYC Municipal Archives; bottom, © Matthew Klein; *page 118:* top, Courtesy of NYC Municipal Archives; bottom, Courtesy of the Gracie Mansion Conservancy; *page 119:* top, The Alpha Workshops; bottom, Drake Design Associates. Photograph by William Waldron; *page 120:* © Hagstrom Map Company, Inc., H-2218; *page 124:* © 2003 N.Y.P. Holdings Inc., D/B/A New York Post; *page 125:* Courtesy of NYC Municipal Archives; *page 126:* Courtesy of NYC Municipal Archives; *page 127:* Courtesy of the Gracie Mansion Conservancy; *page 128:* © 2003 N.Y.P. Holdings Inc., D/B/A New York Post; *page 129:* top, Courtesy of the Gracie Mansion Conservancy; bottom, Courtesy of Paula Perlini Inc.; *pages 130–1:* Courtesy of Paula Perlini Inc.; *pages 132–3:* Courtesy of the Gracie Mansion Conservancy; *page 134:* Courtesy of the Gracie Mansion Conservancy; *page 135:* Courtesy of the Gracie Mansion Conservancy; *page 136:* Courtesy of the Gracie Mansion Conservancy; *page 137:* Courtesy of the Gracie Mansion Conservancy; *page 138:* Courtesy of the New-York Historical Society; *page 139:* © 2003 N.Y.P. Holdings Inc., D/B/A New York Post; *page 140:* The Library of Congress; *page 141:* Courtesy of the Gracie Mansion Conservancy; *page 142:* Courtesy of the Gracie Mansion Conservancy; *page 143:* left, Courtesy of the Gracie Mansion Conservancy; right, Drake Design Associates. Photograph by William Waldron; *page 145:* Courtesy of Albert Hadley; *page 146:* Courtesy of Paula Perlini Inc.; *page 147:* © John M. Hall; *pages 148–9:* © John M. Hall; *page 150:* Courtesy of Maureen Hackett; *page 151:* Courtesy of Maureen Hackett; *page 152:* Courtesy of Maureen Hackett; *page 153:* Courtesy of Maureen Hackett; *page 155:* top, Drake Design Associates; bottom, Drake Design Associates. Photograph by Eric Laignel; *page 156:* Drake Design Associates. Photograph by William Waldron; *page 157:* © Matthew Klein; *page 158:* © Matthew Klein; *page 159:* left and bottom, © Matthew Klein; right, Courtesy of Gordon Roth; *page 160:* © Matthew Klein; *page 161:* Office of the Mayor, Photo Unit, City of New York; *pages 162–3:* Madeleine Doering; *page 164:* Office of the Mayor, Photo Unit, City of New York; *page 165:* Madeleine Doering; *pages 166–7:* Madeleine Doering; *page 169:* Drake Design Associates. Photograph by William Waldron; *page 171:* Drake Design Associates. Photograph by William Waldron; *pages 172–3:* Madeleine Doering; *page 174:* Drake Design Associates. Photograph by William Waldron; *page 175:* Drake Design Associates. Photograph by William Waldron; *pages 176–7:* Drake Design Associates. Photographs by William Waldron; *pages 178–9:* Madeleine Doering; *page 180:* Madeleine Doering; *page 181:* Drake Design Associates. Photograph by William Waldron; *page 182:* Drake Design Associates. Photograph by William Waldron; *page 183:* Drake Design Associates. Photograph by William Waldron; *page 184:* Drake Design Associates. Photograph by William Waldron; *page 185:* Drake Design Associates. Photograph by William Waldron; *page 187:* The City of New York Department of Parks & Recreation, Capital Projects Division, Map File

Gracie Mansion Conservancy

CURRENT

Patricia E. Harris, *Chair*

Brooke Astor

Adrian Benepe

Diane M. Coffey, *Founding Member*

Oscar de la Renta

Kate D. Levin

Josie Natori

Patricia Newburger

Carroll Petrie

Dianne Pilgrim, *Founding Member*

Charles Platt, *Founding Member*

Frederick Schaffer

Pam B. Schafler

Audrey Smaltz

Robert Tierney

Elizabeth Weymouth

Susan Danilow, *Director*

Diana M. Carroll,
    Assistant Director and Curator

PAST MEMBERS

Joan K. Davidson, *Founding Chair*

Laurie Beckelman

James R. Brigham, Jr.

Mary Schmidt Campbell

Luis Cancel

Schuyler G. Chapin

Adrian W. DeWind

Mrs. David N. Dinkins

Barbara J. Fife

Betsy Gotbaum

Donna Hanover

William Josephson

Deborah Krulewich

Noonie Marx

Bernard Mendik

Gene A. Norman

Neil Penkower

Sherida Paulsen

Leon Queller

Jennifer Raab

F. William Reindel

Emily Malino Scheuer

Richard B. Solomon

Henry J. Stern

Lothar Steifel

Ann F. Thomas

E. Thomas Williams

Index

Page numbers in *italics* refer
to illustrations and photographs

About the Author

Ellen Stern has been a writer and editor at *New York*, *GQ*, and the *New York Daily News*. Her books include *Best Bets*, *Once Upon a Telephone*, *Sister Sets*, and *Threads* (with fashion designer Joseph Abboud). She lives in New York City.

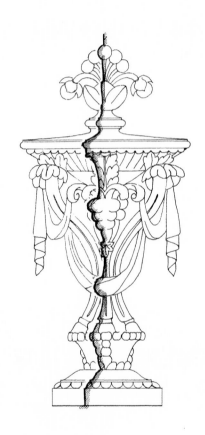